Dior
in
VOGUE

Dior
IN
VOGUE

BRIGID KEENAN
FOREWORD BY
MARGOT FONTEYN

OCTOPUS BOOKS

ACKNOWLEDGMENTS
I am grateful to Madame Raymonde Zehnacker and Madame Cathérine Dior for sharing their memories with me, and to the House of Dior for generously allowing me to use their archives. I would like to thank Alex Kroll for his unfailing good humour and enterprise, Jane Mulvagh for her adept research, and Jorn Langberg of Christian Dior-London for his valuable help.

I am also grateful to *Paris Match* for the use of their files and permission to reproduce the photographs on pages 8, 13 above, 25 and 181.

Finally I should like to thank my husband and daughters for putting up so pleasantly with an author in the family.

CAPTIONS
PAGE 1: Christian Dior by Snowdon who tells this story: 'In the Fifties Audrey Withers, the Editor of *Vogue*, sent me to photograph Dior. She gave me detailed instructions: "I want a picture that will capture his whole glittering empire, *everything* he has done and designed for women in the world," she said. I imagined having to do a great montage of stockings and scent and clothes, but she continued, "I want you to go to his home in the South of France and," she paused, "I think the only thing that will sum up all his achievement . . . is to photograph him in close-up against a perfectly plain white background."'
PAGE 2: Dior's H line evening dress with the 'Tudor' bodice. Spring 1954. COFFIN.
RIGHT: This beautiful black wool dress had a fitted bodice extending into a bell skirt, the décolletage trimmed with a wide collar rising to points on the shoulders. Autumn 1957. KLEIN.

This book first published 1981 by
Octopus Books Limited
59 Grosvenor Street
London W1

ISBN 0 7064 1634 1

Produced by Mandarin Publishers Limited
22a Westlands Road, Quarry Bay, Hong Kong

Printed in Hong Kong

For my mother and father
with love

CONTENTS

FOREWORD

Christian Dior! How well I remember the first time I heard that name. 'Christian who?', I asked and they repeated: 'Dior, D-I-O-R.' I thought it sounded strange, not at all like a couturier: it did not seem to have the ring of the great names – Chanel, Balenciaga, Worth or Molyneux. But it reached the highest rank and came to reign over fashion.

Dior restored grace and elegance to women's dress after the depressingly severe styles of wartime. The curious thing is how easily one's eye grows accustomed to any current fashion, no matter how outlandish. Like most people during the Forties I happily regarded the square shoulders, skimpy skirts and platform shoes as very smart. Then along came Christian Dior's 'New Look', with its feminine lines, small waists and full skirts that were very much longer than anything we had seen for years. There were even some padded hips to accentuate the waistline.

I was lucky enough to be more or less the same size as one of his favourite models, Vicki, and at the end of each season I was able to buy one of the model dresses made on her. From the first Collection I had the simple black outfit called 'Daisy'. The skirt was bell-shaped with three or four horizontal pleats encircling it at intervals and it reached below the calf. The jacket was very close-fitting but filled out with a peplum over the hips. I must admit that I felt a little strange the first day or two but I was soon converted and never looked back. I still have some beautiful evening models.

Reading Brigid Keenan's description of the mounting nervous tension leading up to a new Collection, and of Dior becoming at such times almost physically ill, I was reminded of Frederick Ashton creating a new ballet with the same degree of suffering, the same strain of selecting what to add and where to eliminate and the same necessity to somehow find the magic within himself. After the first exercise of creation comes the process of assessing and re-assessing to try to reach perfection and this continues right up until the show goes on. If it is a ballet it can last for many years but fashion has a butterfly existence: in a few months it is over, dead and gone, and its creator must be ready on the appointed day with his new line. Time won't wait for him, nor will the world of *Vogue*!

This book is a fine salute to the shy genius who crammed what seemed like a lifetime of creativity into the ten short years of his reign over the kingdom of fashion. In that brief time he influenced millions of people the world over in the most peaceful and benign manner, and that seems to me to be a great and very worthwhile achievement indeed.

MARGOT FONTEYN ARIAS

The sequined tulle of the ball dress, *right*, was made by Madame Brossin de Méré with beads and sequins on the petalled layers. HORST.

THE GENTLE GENIUS

One autumn day in 1948, passers-by in the Rue Lepic in Paris came upon a shocking sight: an attractive, well-dressed young woman was being violently attacked by a couple of elderly harridans who seemed intent on tearing the clothes off her back. The scuffle must have attracted quite a crowd, and among the onlookers was a photographer, Walter Carone, whose picture of the drama has been used again and again all over the world, and has now become part of the Christian Dior legend. For the young woman was set upon only because she was wearing clothes inspired by Dior's New Look, a fashion that had aroused such controversy when it was launched the previous year that there had even been anti-Dior demonstrations. The ugly incident in the Rue Lepic did not therefore come as a great surprise to anyone.

It is possible, of course, that the attack was set up as a publicity stunt, but the House of Dior has always denied any such thing and it is difficult to believe that the gentle Christian Dior would have been a party to such a crude idea. In any case, since newspapers and magazines of the time (and since) never questioned the photograph and used it in good faith, it seems to me that, true or false, it still serves as a vivid reminder of how the New Look raised people's blood pressure and stirred their passions less than 35 years ago.

Five years later, an article appeared in the French magazine *Paris Match* that nicely shows the power that Christian Dior had by now achieved over his public, not only over what they wore, but their imaginations as well. In July 1953 Dior had raised hemlines by a bare two inches. Here is the wonderfully dramatic tale that the London correspondent of *Paris Match* unfolded then:

'The eight million inhabitants of London were sleeping. That day, July 27, 1953, had been extremely beautiful. There had been no hint of what was to come. In Fleet Street, where the powerful newspapers have their offices, the night news editors were dozing. In front of the ultra-modern glass and plastic building of *The Daily Express* a courier from one of the news agencies parked his motorbike. He went in and delivered a small package to one of the messengers who took it up to the desk of the Editor-in-Chief. The Editor read the contents, rose, and cried, "HOLD THE FRONT PAGE!" The message was datelined Paris. It was as brief as a military communiqué: "Christian Dior today showed his Winter Collection. Dresses stop just below the knee." Throughout Fleet Street every Editor-in-Chief picked up his telephone and called Paris. "Cable," they ordered their correspondents, "Cable the whole story. Length unlimited." At dawn all England read the incredible news on the newspaper front pages across two, three and even four columns...'

The world's Press had an extraordinary ten-year-long love affair with Dior. It began when he opened the doors of his couture house to show the New Look, and it never flagged, for Dior never

The House of Dior at night before a Collection – lights ablaze, employees working furiously.

failed to design clothes that were newsworthy as well as beautiful and in writing about them, the journalists turned their creator into a legend – the most famous fashion designer who has ever lived.

Vogue magazine was just as enthusiastic as the rest of the Press, but being a fashion magazine it had a certain responsibility to its readers. No one can pretend that fashion writing is nothing if not flowery, but *Vogue* could certainly not afford to give in to the flights of fancy that *Paris Match* and others could indulge in. Their editors spotted Dior's genius immediately and supported him through every controversy, but they had to lead their readers through the intricacies of fashion changes and explain how to wear them. Most important of all for fashion history, *Vogue* documented in photographs and sketches the most influential clothes in each Collection, the ones that would be bought and copied by the newly-emerging ready-to-wear industry, that women would actually end up *wearing*. It is *Vogue's* detailed, blow-by-blow accounts of his Collections that form the basis for this book on the great Christian Dior.

In appearance, Dior was hardly the stuff of legends. His hair was transparently thin, he was plump, gentle, shy and melancholy. He had a habit of folding his hands and bowing his head a little to one side. Cecil Beaton observed that he looked 'like a bland country curate made out of pink marzipan'. He was middle-aged before success came to him – he celebrated his forty-second birthday three weeks before his first Collection – and, though of course he could not know it, time was running out already. There was to be no old age for Dior: his death came suddenly at the age of 52.

Christian Dior was more aware than anyone else that his looks were a bit dull compared to his glittering new reputation: 'I could not help thinking that I cut a sorry figure – a well-fed gentleman in the Parisian's favourite neutral-coloured suit . . .' he wrote in his memoirs, gently mocking himself. 'I wondered if I ought to transform myself, in order not to disappoint my public? Perhaps I ought to go on a diet, and renounce not only greed, but everything which makes life worth living. I splashed out timidly with a flower in my buttonhole. I ordered several more suits from my

tailor, put myself in the hands of a masseur, and almost immediately gave the whole project up. I decided that the gap between imagination and reality was too wide. With relief, I sank back into my own shell, which had come to fit me very comfortably after so many years.'

Given the way he felt about his appearance, it was not surprising that Dior flinched from cameras, but from 1947 he was a celebrity and there was always someone lying in wait. On one occasion he found a photographer hiding in his own sitting room: the young man had bribed the concierge to let him in, and Dior took pity on him and allowed him to take some pictures. But another time, in England, he locked himself in a restaurant lavatory rather than run the gauntlet

Dior's pretty, elegant mother, Madeleine, *below*, at the Deauville races. She was, he said, his inspiration for the New Look, of which the dress, *opposite*, sketched by Nobili in Maxim's restaurant, was typical.

of photographers waiting outside. When Dior died in Italy he was with Madame Raymonde, his right-hand woman at work and his closest friend, who had always shielded him from such encounters. Distraught by his sudden death, Madame Raymonde could only think of continuing to protect her beloved employer from the heartless hordes of *paparazzi* – the photographers who besieged their hotel, and even climbed up drainpipes in their determination to snatch deathbed pictures of the famous designer.

MEMORIES

If Dior's looks were at odds with his image, his early background was still more so. His father had inherited the unglamorous family business of making fertilizers. Dior's great-great-grandfather had begun it in 1832, and the Diors had prospered ever since. Now they were a well-to-do family, highly respected in Granville, Normandy, where their large villa stood, a little outside the town, on top of a high cliff overlooking the sea. Dior described this house as 'perfectly hideous' but he remembered it with great affection and always said that his favourite colour combination of pink and grey was first inspired by the pink roughcast and grey gravelling that decorated the outside of the villa.

The Dior house was bought by the town of Granville in the Thirties – not, obviously, for Dior's sake, but to accommodate locally-based naval officers. The land around it, which was once all park and pinewoods ('like a virgin forest to us children', said Dior wistfully) has been encroached upon by new buildings, but in 1976 Granville paid tribute to their famous son by erecting a bust of Dior and creating a public garden in the grounds of what used to be his home.

Dior's father was a good, solid Norman: sturdily built and with a bulging tummy that betrayed the family failing – love of good food. But his mother, Madeleine, came from Anjou and was slim, elegant and attractive. Dior loved her more than anyone, confiding to Madame Raymonde that it was memories of his mother that prompted him to create the New Look. His mother, with her tiny, corseted, hand-span waist and tight-fitting bodices; with her full, rustling silk skirts and her creamy smooth shoulders in the low-cut evening dresses of the period; his mother, who would come and kiss him goodnight before she went out, leaving the smell of her perfume lingering in his room to send him happily to sleep.

The skimpy, masculine clothes that women wore during the Second World War were anathema to Dior: 'hideous, repellent', he called them, and he yearned for women to recover their femininity again, and for their clothes to regain the kind of charm and elegance that his mother's had. When his New Look succeeded beyond his wildest dreams, he confessed that revenge on the ugly wartime outfits was part of the pleasure he felt in its success.

Dior was born in Granville on January 21, 1905. He was to be the second son and there were to be five children in the family altogether, another brother and two sisters. Of all of them he was fondest of Cathérine, the youngest, and they remained close until his death. (She and her sister are still alive, though all the Dior sons are now dead.) The five children in the family led a sheltered, well-ordered life, with servants to help with the house and German *fräuleins* to help with the children. Dior described himself as 'a very good, very well brought-up little boy'.

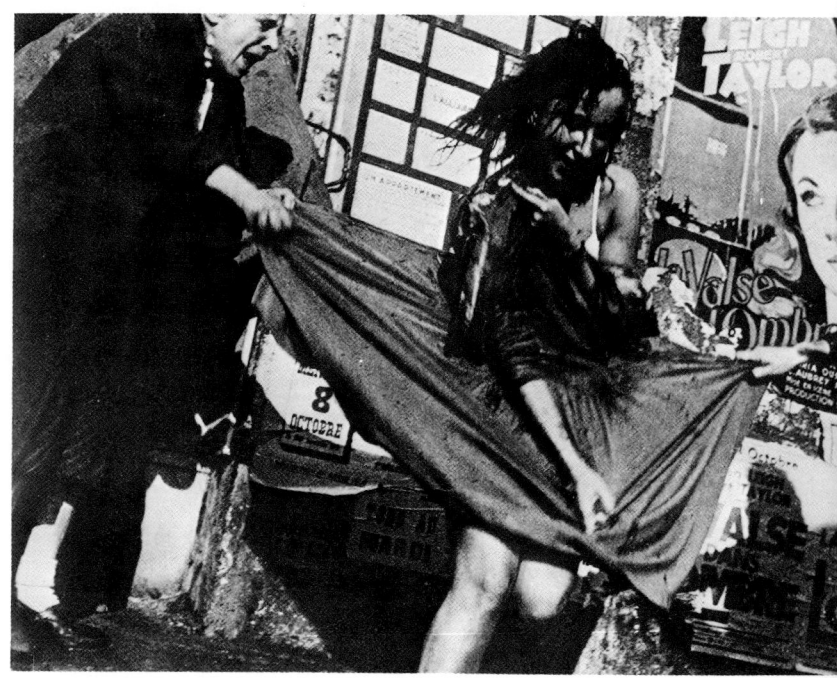

A final consultation in the grand Louis Quinze salon, *opposite left*. The crowded showing of the New Look, *opposite right*. Note the clumpy shoes and short skirts of the audience.

B anners greeted Dior's arrival in Chicago soon after the New Look Collection in 1947, *above*. Enraged housewives, *top right*, try to rip the Dior dress off an early wearer in Paris. CARONE.

It was in Granville when Dior was 14 that he was given the first clue about his future: a gypsy fortune teller at a local fête read his palm, and what she told him Dior never forgot. 'You will suffer poverty, but women are lucky for you and through them you will achieve success. You will make a great deal of money out of them and you will have to travel widely.' This all seemed hilariously far-fetched to the family, especially the part about travelling, for Dior was so timid and unadventurous that he would even make a fuss about going to see a friend. (In later life travel became one of his pleasures – but not by aeroplane. He was terrified of flying. Just once Madame Raymonde persuaded him to fly to New York but, as luck would have it, everything went wrong and the trip took 24 hours. Dior, she smiles, never forgave her for it.)

Cathérine Dior remembers more positive clues as to his future career as a dress designer. Once a year the casino at Granville would hold a costume ball and young Christian Dior took enormous pains designing his own outfits. 'He would sketch costumes and an elderly maid of ours would sew them for him. Once he went as Neptune in a long skirt of green rafia with a bodice made of sea shells painted gold . . . He always adored drawing and even sketched on the walls of his bathroom.'

As a schoolboy Dior used to get into trouble for doodling ladies' feet in high-heeled shoes in the margins of his exercise books.

The Dior family moved to Paris when Christian was five. They took an apartment in Passy, the smart sixteenth *arrondissement*. It was decorated in what Dior called 'Louis Seize/Passy' style, which meant high-ceilinged rooms with plaster-panelled walls painted palest grey, white wood-work and white enamelled furniture. There were crystal chandeliers, potted palms and elegant doors with small panes of bevelled glass. Dior remembered that home with nostalgia and affection too, and when it came to decorating his couture house years later, he chose to try to reproduce the elegant rooms of his parents' home.

The House of Dior has expanded vastly since the heady days when Christian Dior first took on number 30 Avenue Montaigne, but the Dior style of décor remains exactly the same whether in Paris, London, New York or Caracas. By now it should be called 'Louis Seize/Passy/Dior', so distinctive has it become – always the grey and white panelled walls, the giant palms, the crystal chandeliers, the plush grey carpets – and everywhere the scent of *Miss Dior* perfume with which the staff traditionally spray the rooms.

The Dior family were on holiday in Granville when the First World War broke out. They stayed there and, it seems, remained fairly uninvolved until they moved back to Paris in 1916. Dior was now supposed to be studying for his *baccalauréat* and thinking of a career, but he was not quite the docile, malleable boy he had been and, increasingly, he wanted to escape from his comfortable middle-class life and explore other worlds.

He suggested to his parents that he should study Fine Arts, but they forbade any such thing. They did not want their son living in some sort of bohemian *demi-monde*: he was to have something solid behind him. He was duly enrolled at the School of Political Science with a view to eventually becoming a diplomat, but apart from attending the necessary classes, he lived his life more or less as he pleased.

The Twenties were tremendously exciting years for a young man interested in the arts in Paris. Dior was 20 years old when the famous *Arts*

The simple, oak-beamed dining room, *above*, of Dior's mill house, Le Coudret. Dior's Paris house drawing room, *left*, with Sèvres jardinière and Aubusson carpet. DENNEY.

Decoratifs exhibition was held (from which, of course, Art Deco got its name). He was enthralled by the surge of new ideas in art, music, architecture and literature. 'I explored the four corners of the new Paris, alive with inventions, cosmopolitan, intelligent and rich in truly new ideas.'

Eventually, Dior persuaded his parents to allow him to drop out of *Sciences Po* (as it was nicknamed) and study musical composition instead. Soon he found himself part of a charmed circle of talented people: Henri Sauguet and Francis Poulenc, composers; Max Jacob and Christian Bérard, artists; Pierre Gaxotte, the historian, and other, lesser-known youngsters. Sauguet christened their little group *Le Club*, and at their meeting place, a bar in the Rue Tronchet called the Tip Toes, they would spend hours eating pastries, gossiping and exchanging ideas.

Dior was still rather timid, and few of the group suspected that his career would ultimately outshine the best of theirs. Photographer André Ostier, who was one of the group, says now that Dior's extraordinary talent for fancy dress should, perhaps, have given them a clue. Fancy dress parties and charades were a Twenties craze and Dior, apparently, was a positive wizard at invention. 'With three pieces of velvet and an old hat he could produce a fabulous costume,' says Ostier.

In due course Dior was called up for military service, but was sent to join a regiment stationed at Versailles – and from there, of course, he could still spend time with his friends in Paris. To his parents' horror, he announced on his discharge from the army that he intended to start an art gallery in partnership with a friend. Terrible rows and arguments followed, which often ended with Dior calling his father 'a dirty bourgeois', stamping out of the apartment and slamming the door.

In the end, however, his parents agreed to finance his share of the gallery so long as the good name of Dior was not disgraced by being used in the title of the firm. Dior and his friend set up shop in a seedy alleyway off the Rue de la Boétie and there they were reasonably successful in

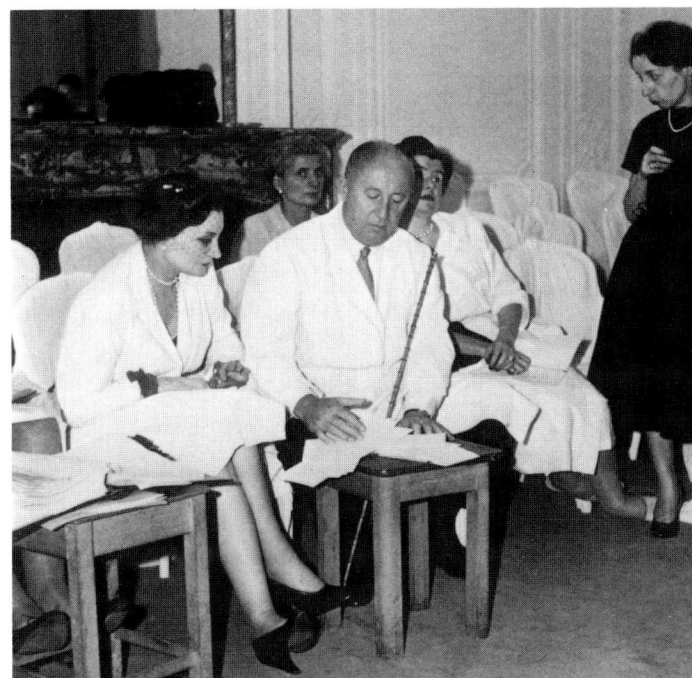

Dior at work: choosing fabrics, altering a hem, and checking final details.

selling the works of painters they admired, or knew, or both: Picasso, Braque, Matisse, Dufy, Christian Bérard and Salvador Dali among them.

This was the year 1928 and Dior was to look back on it as a high point in his life. 'That wonderful time,' he called it, 'when our youth ran free and everything and anything seemed likely to succeed.'

DREAMS AND SCHEMES

Although Christian Dior was a practising Catholic who did not like to miss Mass and communion on Sundays, he was also a remarkably superstitious man, forever seeing omens and portents all around him. He consulted fortune tellers regularly – perhaps the gypsy in Granville had given him the taste – and especially before making a decision he considered important. In fact, it was Madame Delahaye, his favourite fortune teller in Paris, who bullied him into accepting the opportunity to start up his own House when it came. 'Nothing anyone will offer you later will compare with the chance which is open to you now,' she told him. At the same time, Madame Raymonde visited another fortune teller – to get a second opinion, as it were. She saw a particularly secret and mysterious old lady known as 'The Grandmother' who, apparently, went into raptures at what she saw in the future for Dior: 'This house is going to revolutionize fashion,' she told her. Bizarre though it sounds, these two fortune tellers really were behind Dior's decision to open up his own couture house.

Luck, Dior always said, was the most important ingredient in his life and he certainly had generous helpings of it, both good and bad. Curiously, the bad luck proved to be as useful to him as the good, for by *not* allowing him to find his niche in life, it saved him for that great moment in 1947 when he became the right man for the right time. If Fate had simply allowed him to continue as a reasonably successful art dealer, he would never have known the power and glory he achieved as a couturier (though he might, on the other hand, have lived longer). The years he spent floundering about trying to find himself made him, eventually, more appealing to the public too, for there is no doubt that we all enjoy a rags-to-riches story best and prefer to see success hard won.

In 1930 a huge mirror fell off a wall in the Diors' Paris apartment, shattering into a thousand pieces on the floor. Dior was appalled and prophesied that nothing but disaster for the family could follow this worst-of-all omens. Oddly enough, everything did seem to go wrong from that time. Dior's brother was struck down by mental illness and then their beloved mother, Madeleine, died suddenly. In the meantime Dior's father had invested all his money in a property development scheme which suddenly collapsed early the following year. More or less overnight, the Dior family became poor.

The American stock market crash and the great recession were being felt everywhere, Paris had become a gloomy place and Dior, unwilling to face reality, took himself off to Russia on a sort of package tour for architects. That proved to be a fairly grim experience too, and on his return, Dior was greeted by the news that his partner in the art gallery was bankrupt and that his father and sister had moved back to Normandy.

He was now 26 years old with no home or family in Paris and found himself without a job, prospects, or money. There were some paintings left from the gallery, but money was tight and he found it difficult to sell them. For many months he continued to live a hand-to-mouth existence in Paris, but then he fell ill and his friends became seriously worried. Somehow they raised enough money to send him away to recover, and Dior spent the next year recuperating in Spain. His health improved, but he was never a very fit man afterwards.

On his return to Paris he stayed with a friend, Jean Ozenne, a freelance dress designer, who encouraged him to try his hand at fashion drawing. One historic day, Dior sold six of his sketches to a newspaper for the princely sum of 20 francs each – it was the first money he had ever earned through his own creative talent.

By now Dior's father and sister had gone to live in Callian, a tiny village in the Var, and Dior had been able to give them a little financial help, thanks to the sale of a Dufy painting. Taking the tools of his new trade – paper, pencils and paints – Dior retired to Callian to build up a portfolio of sketches. He sold many of them to the newspaper *Le Figaro* and to Agnès, the milliner, but it was another couple of years before he was actually offered a full-time job as a designer, with the couturier Robert Piguet. Just as he was beginning to do well in his new career, however, Fate intervened again: war broke out, Dior was mobilized and sent off to work on the land.

When the French were defeated, Dior was discharged from military service and made his way back to his father and sister in Callian, where he stayed for a year growing vegetables to sell in the local markets. Returning to Paris, he found that Piguet had grown impatient and had hired someone to replace him. But this was the hand of Fate too, for Dior fortunately found employment with Lucien Lelong, the man who, as *doyen* of the Paris couturiers during the war, had prevented the Germans from moving the French couture to Berlin or Vienna.

Lucien Lelong's house was much bigger than Piguet's and there Dior was able to learn far more about the business; there too he met Madame Raymonde, who was to become his right-hand helper.

Lucien Lelong did no designing himself, but under his direction this was carried out by Dior and another young man who was also to become a famous couturier – Pierre Balmain. Madame Raymonde liked them both in different ways: 'Pierre was a love, full of fun, always playful and fooling about, but Dior enchanted me. He was the opposite: very calm, very well-mannered, very gentlemanly. Even then you could see that he had immense talent – when we went through their sketches it was somehow always Dior's that were new, full of ideas, in advance.'

But all this newfound happiness was soon to be blighted by anxiety and sorrow. Cathérine Dior, who had become an active member of the Resistance, was arrested in Paris by the Gestapo and sent to the notorious Ravensbrück Concentration Camp. Until the camp was liberated by the Russians ten months later no one knew where she was. Then, unrecognizable, thin and gaunt, she returned to Paris where Dior, full of joy and love, gave her new clothes from Lelong. 'It was the only time in my life,' she smiled wryly, 'that I was able to fit into his model sized dresses.'

After four happy years at Lelong, Christian Dior was approached by the great French textile

millionaire Marcel Boussac – 'King Cotton', as he was known in France. He was offered the task of re-vamping a small couture house called *Gaston et Philippe*, but when he went to inspect the new venture, he immediately decided against the job. 'No,' he blurted out to Boussac at their first fateful meeting. 'What I really want to do is not to resurrect *Gaston*, but create a new couture house under my own name, in a district of my own choosing. I want a house in which every single thing will be new: from the *ambiance* and the staff, down to the furniture and even the address.' Almost despite himself and his chronic shyness, Dior went on to describe the house of his dreams: 'It would be small and secluded, with very few workrooms; within them the work would be done according to the highest traditions of *haute couture*; the clothes, which would give an impression of simplicity, would in fact involve elaborate

workmanship and would be aimed at a *clientèle* of really elegant women. . .'

Boussac was impressed, as much by Dior's sober and sensible appearance – 'he breathed good taste' – as he was by his words. 'What convinced me about Dior was that he had a very precise idea about what he wanted to do, and he had paid attention to every little detail,' Boussac later told his aides, who were taken aback by this rapid decision to back Dior. Dior was shocked too, so much so that he panicked and sent Boussac a telegram calling the whole thing off. It was then that he rushed to Madame Delahaye, his fortune teller, who urged him into the right decision.

At this point, the lease on a house that Dior had always liked, number 30 Avenue Montaigne, came up for sale. Boussac secured it and in September 1946 Dior left Lelong to start his own business – the House of Christian Dior.

Bouché's sketch shows Dior's Directrice walking between the fashion experts; in the foreground, Edmonde Charles-Roux, Cathy McManus and Jessica Daves, all from *Vogue*.

THE THREE MOTHERS

Dior had confided in Madame Raymonde all through his negotiations with Boussac, and he had begged her to come with him. 'But I had to think,' says Madame Raymonde. 'I had, after all, been with Lelong for 25 years.' Eventually she agreed, as he had known she would, and became indispensible both to Dior personally and to the workings of his house. 'My second self' is what Dior called her.

With Madame Raymonde at his right hand, Dior began selecting the rest of his team with, as it turned out, an unerring eye. His work-room chief, or technical director, Madame Marguerite, was brought in from a rival couture house. Her job, to interpret Dior's sketches and turn them into clothes, was vital, for Dior had never learned to cut or sew himself. Unlike Balenciaga, who was a technician of extraordinary skill, he preferred to remain one step removed from the actual making up of the garments: to become too involved, he felt, would destroy his vision.

In Madame Marguerite Dior had found a per-fectionist like himself. 'Nothing is ever beautiful enough, or perfect enough for her,' he said. 'She will stitch, unstitch, cut, cut again, a hundred times. . . If the world came to an end while she was poring over a dress I really do not believe she would notice it.'

Next, Dior hired Madame Bricard, who had previously worked with Molyneux, a designer whom Dior admired enormously. Her role is rather hard to define: in theory she was supposed to be in charge of hats, but she was really there to

act as inspiration – a kind of Muse. 'Dior always had a need for beautiful things around him,' says Madame Raymonde, 'and he loved to look at Madame Bricard.' Dior himself said: 'Madame Bricard is one of those people, increasingly rare, who makes elegance their sole *raison d'être*. I knew that her presence in my house would inspire me towards creation.' Their collaboration worked: Madame Bricard's extravagant taste and extra-ordinary chic made the perfect counter-balance to Dior's more down-to-earth temperament.

Madame Raymonde, Madame Marguerite and Madame Bricard came to be known as 'the three mothers', for though their jobs were to organize, interpret and inspire Dior, they mothered him too, especially Madame Raymonde. Neverthe-less, the House of Dior was run on old-fashioned,

Dior's clients included some of the most famous actresses in the world, such as Jane Russell, *right*, and Olivia de Havilland, *left*.

formal lines, and Dior invariably addressed each one as Madame, while to his staff he was always *le Patron*.

The only member of staff appointed by Marcel Boussac was the director of the house, in charge of administration and finance: Jacques Rouet was an excellent choice, for he is there to this day.

Cleaners, doormen, seamstresses, secretaries, saleswomen, and so on, now had to be found, until the staff numbered 60 in all. Only six of those were mannequins, but Dior valued them almost more than anyone else: 'They alone can bring my clothes to life,' he said. He believed that no amount of schooling could produce a star. 'A good mannequin is born, not made. Like successful dresses, born mannequins are elegant without effort.' To be a Dior mannequin in the Fifties was a prestigious job, and many of Dior's favourites became quite famous: Alla, the aloof, impassive oriental; Lucky, who, according to Dior, did not merely wear clothes but *acted* them; France, the epitome of Parisian elegance; and Victoire, who caused a storm of protest when Dior hired her because of her student-like, Left Bank look.

But all that was later. To find his first team of six girls, Dior put advertisements in the Paris newspapers – with hilarious results. 'As luck would have it,' Dior recalled in his memoirs, 'I chose the exact moment when a new law was forcing certain famous Paris brothels to close.' Dior, and a horrified Madame Raymonde, found themselves interviewing dozens and dozens of call-girls, but he was determined to go through with every interview – just in case. He found many of the girls extraordinarily pretty, but none had what he called the 'presence' and the 'bearing' to become a Dior model: in the end he found those elsewhere.

The opening day for Dior's first Collection had been fixed for February 12, 1947. Decoration had begun on the house itself and in December Dior disappeared to the country to create his Collection.

His New Look designs called for unusually intricate workmanship and a return to sewing techniques that had gone out of fashion and were almost forgotten. With less than two months to get the Collection ready, an untried staff, and not enough space, things became frantic. Work was done on the stairs, in corridors; one of the key workroom ladies collapsed with nerves and at one trying-on session a model passed out in Dior's arms.

A tremendous aura of secrecy shrouded the whole house, for if details of a Collection leaked in advance, it could spell financial ruin for a couture house. Which manufacturer would *pay* to come and see a Collection if he could copy it without? All sorts of precautions had to be taken to thwart spies both inside and outside the house; sketches were meticulously numbered, all rejected garments were locked away, dresses were always carried around the house wrapped in cloth, and if a stranger came near, sheets would instantly be flung over everything. During the showing of a Collection, the audience was strictly forbidden to sketch the clothes. A discreet watch was kept to make sure no one was committing this crime, and once Dior himself came out from behind the scenes to escort a red-faced woman to the door and tear up her notebook in front of everyone.

While the New Look was in preparation even Marcel Boussac did not know what was going on, and he was rapidly becoming as nervous as everyone else. But the night before the Collection he was reassured: 'I went home and found in the hall a bouquet of orchids, quite beautifully arranged. They had been sent by Dior. I had never seen such an exquisite arrangement in my life. I went upstairs to Madame Boussac's room and said: ''Don't worry about tomorrow, there is not a florist in the world who could have created such a beautiful bunch of flowers as the one I have just seen – tomorrow *must* be an immense success.'' '

On the morning of February 12, Dior arrived very early to find the carpet still being laid and the florists still at work on vast arrangements of flowers. Although work had been going on all night, the whole house was in an uproar.

By some miracle the show began at 10.30, as scheduled, and Dior took up his traditional position behind the grey curtains leading into the big showroom. From there he could cast a last glance over each mannequin before she made her entrance, and from there he tried to judge the audience's response. Later they were all to become experts at this, but on that first morning, exhausted with tension, nerves strung to breaking point, he could not believe – dared not believe –

the applause when it came. But soon the audience's approval was unmistakeable: every garment was being greeted with loud clapping and cries of *bravo*! When the show ended, in a tumult of enthusiasm, Madame Marguerite, Madame Bricard and Christian Dior stood silently in the models' dressing room and just looked at each other, dumbfounded. 'Then Raymonde, crying with joy, came to look for us, to take us into the big salon where we were greeted with a salvo of applause. As long as I live, whatever triumphs I win, nothing will ever exceed my feelings at that supreme moment.'

CREATING A COLLECTION

For a man with Dior's personality – gentle, oversensitive, anxious, and with an urgent need to be loved and approved, a career as the most famous dress designer in the world is just what the doctor would *not* have ordered. His friend, the artist Christian Bérard, summed up the dilemma very neatly at a dinner given to celebrate the success of the New Look Collection. 'My dear Christian,' he said in his speech, 'savour this moment of happiness well, for it is unique in your career. Never again will success come to you so easily; for tomorrow begins the anguish of living up to and, if possible, surpassing yourself.'

No Dior Collection was ever born in serenity. The creation of each one brought anguish and stress, violent ups and downs, tears, tantrums, hysteria and panic for Dior, as well as his staff. Though he wrote lightheartedly of the trials of being a fashion designer, it is not generally known how much he suffered because of his career. From time to time it made him physically ill, and it probably led to his early death. 'Eight days before each Collection he would be sick with worry and nerves and lack of confidence,' recalls Madame Raymonde, who became at these times his guardian angel. She would follow him round with a medicine chest, acting as a buffer between Dior and his staff, shielding him from any unpleasantness.

Two years after the opening, the pressures became too great and Dior could not cope any longer. He summoned Madame Raymonde in the middle of the night and she hurried to his home with a doctor, who diagnosed 'tremendous fatigue'.

Dior was depressed, exhausted and ill; it took him six months to recover his spirits and from that time until his death Madame Raymonde rarely left his side.

The creation of a Collection would begin calmly enough with the fabric manufacturers coming to 30 Avenue Montaigne to show their new cloths. Dior would make his selection there and then, several weeks before he did any designing. Occasionally he would ask a manufacturer to create a special fabric. Once in Switzerland, for instance, he had been admiring the curved slate tiles on the roofs of the old houses. 'How I wish you could make a cloth that looks like those,' he mentioned to Madame Brossin de Méré, a famous fabric designer, with whom he was walking. Three months later she brought him some organdie exquisitely embroidered to look like the tiles he had loved.

When the fabrics had been chosen, Dior (with Madame Raymonde) would take a short holiday 'to change my ideas and to help me break with the last Collection'. They often went to Italy, which they both loved.

On his return, Dior would disappear down to the country, to his old mill house near the Forest of Fontainebleau, or, later on, to the château in the Var which he bought for his retirement. There, pockets stuffed with pencils, crayons, notebooks, sharpeners and erasers, he would relax and potter in the garden waiting for inspiration to come. It always did: sometimes an idea would strike him with the force of an electric shock, he said, and these were always the best ones.

Soon, like a man possessed, Dior would be sketching everywhere: on tablecloths, on restaurant bills, in bed and in the bath. (He particularly liked to work in the bath, keeping the temperature up by letting the hot tap trickle in.) At night he would dream of dresses, wake, sketch, and sleep again.

And all the time, the ideas would be taking shape. Sometimes, in order to bring an idea into focus, he would think back to the fabrics he had chosen and visualize his ideas made up in them, or, better still, he would think of a woman he admired, perhaps a client, and imagine her dressed in his new shapes.

After a few days' break, Dior would go over all

the sketches he had done – there could be hundreds – and weed out the least attractive ones. Then he would re-draw and refine his selection and take it to Paris. There, in the meantime, Madame Raymonde, Madame Marguerite and Madame Bricard would have been becoming increasingly nervous. 'As the date drew nearer for a Collection and Monsieur Dior had not shown us anything, I used to get worried that perhaps he had nothing ready. I hesitated to ask him, for that wouldn't have helped. But then one day without warning he would say: "I have something to show you", and he'd lay his drawings out.' Madame Marguerite remembers that Dior, always a showman, would keep the best sketches at the bottom of the pile to show last.

Together they made a final selection of sketches and Madame Marguerite would hand these out to each of the workrooms. The workroom foreman or forewoman would be briefed as to what kind of client would buy each garment, how she would wear it and on what occasion, for Dior believed that a successful dress must have a personality. To this end, every Dior dress had a name that was specially chosen for it.

Using Dior's sketch as their blueprint, the workrooms would start by making a pattern for the dress in white canvas. This was called a *toile*, and it would be adjusted, re-adjusted, snipped at and fiddled with on a wooden dummy before it was tried on a real mannequin. When the *toiles* were ready, the mannequins modelled them for Dior. At this stage, a dress might have worked beautifully, or perhaps it had possibilities, or it might have come out looking so appalling that Dior would order it to be thrown into the dustbin.

The mannequins' job at this stage in the preparation of a Collection was boring and exhausting. If a dress had possibilities that was worst of all, for it meant standing for hours while Dior, Madame Marguerite and the workroom chief ripped the *toile* to bits and put it together again in a dozen different ways.

Now the moment had come when Dior had to select the fabric that each *toile* would be made in. Dior, Madame Raymonde, Madame Marguerite and Madame Bricard – dressed in their white overalls they looked like a surgeon and his nurses – would assemble once more, together with bales

and bales of cloth. One by one the model girls wearing the *toiles* would come in and stand patiently while perhaps 50 or 100 bales were unrolled and draped over their shoulders to see the effect. Days would pass before all the decisions were made and the staff would totter home each night exhausted. 'Behind each fabric,' Dior once said, 'there are artists, workers, industries, whole towns depending on our choice. We must remember that their efforts deserve to be rewarded.'

At last, the dresses would be cut out in the chosen cloths, made up and presented to Dior once again. At this stage the showing of the Collection was only a couple of weeks away. The tension was mounting each day, and the House of Dior lived on its nerves as the deadline drew

Dior with his dog Bobby. There was always a dress called Bobby in a Dior Collection.

nearer. 'I am in a terrible mood all this time,' Dior confessed. 'My faithful staff tiptoe about the studio, terrified of letting a pin drop, trying to make themselves invisible.'

At long last, three days before the opening show, there would be the dress rehearsal. Yet again the weary staff assembled in the *grand salon* to scrutinize the clothes, and even at this last minute hems could be re-pinned, pockets shifted, collars altered. On the floor boxes overflowed with gloves, jewellery, umbrellas, belts, hats, buttons, ribbons and all sorts of pretty bits and pieces: from these, finishing touches would be chosen for the 175 or so outfits. Dior, pointing with his long baton, quietly directed operations: 'That bow should be more important. It doesn't seem to fasten to anything ... Away with the fur. It clashes with the hat ... Add a black umbrella to it ... It should look more striking, add the flower ... I know what's wrong – it needs two more buttons.'

In the two days left before the opening show an eerie silence fell over the House of Dior: everyone was working flat out and there was no more time for nerves or tantrums. In these last hours, Dior retired to his office to work out the price each garment should sell for. He always did this himself, costing the sum from the detailed files kept on every outfit, listing the quantity and price of cloth used, the trimmings and the hours of workmanship that had gone into each one.

Soon the workrooms had sewn the last stitch, completed the last alteration. It was too late now to change anything and, for Dior, these final moments before the first show were agony. 'I want to escape. I am hoping for a sudden catastrophe – even a fatal one – that will prevent the Collection being shown. I want to die ...' But all his fears in the end were needless, for Dior never had a failure on his hands. Of course, some Collections were less successful than others: the graph of sales would dip here and there, but the measure of Dior's talent is that, in ten years, he did not have a single failure.

PRIVATE LIFE, AND DEATH

Dior had never meant to be dynamite. His modest ambition on setting up his own house was simply 'to do my best' and he was astonished to find his first Collection sending shock waves around the world, and he himself a celebrity, literally overnight. 'It was extraordinary, it was like living in a dream. We did not know what had happened,' recalls Madame Raymonde.

Within weeks of his opening, Dior learned that the Texas store Neiman Marcus had awarded him a fashion 'Oscar'. For the sake of the French couture as much as for himself, Dior travelled to America (by the liner *Queen Elizabeth*) for the presentation ceremony. There he found himself facing press conferences – as well as anti-Dior demonstrations – and was amused to be bombarded with the same questions in every city he visited: 'What is the right length for a skirt, Mr Dior? What will be the trend of your next Collection?'

In the autumn of that year he was invited to bring his Collection to Britain for a special show at the Savoy Hotel in London. But on his arrival in the capital there was extra, unexpected excitement. He was asked to put on a special private show at the French Embassy for the Queen of England (now the Queen Mother), her daughter Princess Margaret and the Duchess of Kent – all of them obviously curious to see what the fuss was about. It was a most unusual request, as well as being highly secret. The Dior dresses, wrapped in white cloth, were smuggled out of the service entrance of the Savoy, and it was very much like taking part in a thriller, Dior later recalled.

In due course he received the highest accolade the French government can award one of its citizens, the *Légion d'Honneur*, for his almost single-handed revival of the French couture industry after the War.

Wealth followed closely on the heels of Dior's success, and with the money he made from his first Collection he was able to fulfil his old ambition of having a house in the country. Near a town called Milly on the edge of the Forest of Fontainebleau he found a fifteenth century mill house, which was everything he had ever wanted. Built in stone, with a pretty courtyard, Le Coudret stood on the edge of a river with a rambling garden all around, and he took immense pleasure in restoring it simply and unpretentiously. There were white walls and dark beams, stone-flagged floors, simple furniture gleaming with the patina of age and care, big country cupboards smelling

Dior in an unexpected role – making raspberry liqueur in the kitchen of his old mill house, Le Coudret.

of lavender. Le Coudret became his haven from the hurly-burly of Paris and there he would retreat at weekends and to design his Collections.

Wearing enormous gumboots and a thick, sloppy sweater, he spent hours working in the garden with his dog Bobby at his heels. Henri Sauguet, his friend, once described Bobby as looking like 'a joint of meat that can run', but his master was loyal to him and there was always a dress called Bobby in a Dior Collection. During the summer he loved to arrange vases of the flowers he had grown, or he would put on a vast

chef's apron and make raspberry liqueur with berries from his own canes. In the evenings he would relax simply: sewing a tapestry or playing cards – he was a Canasta fanatic – or playing the piano, at which he excelled. In the kitchen, Madame Denise – the only cook in Dior dresses joked his friends – would prepare delicious meals for him and his guests.

No sooner was Le Coudret organized, than Dior's new-found success forced him to look for a larger and grander place in Paris than the flat in the Rue Royale where he had lived for years, so that he could do the inevitable official entertaining. Nostalgia for his childhood was very strong in Dior, and he was understandably overjoyed to find a house for sale in the Boulevard Jules Sandeau, only a few yards from where his parents' home had been. He could even hear the bell at his old school. Not only that, the house was one they had all known well by sight – a charming, eccentric house that had apparently been built for the mistress of a Russian Grand Duke. He took it immediately and created there a town house as grand and sophisticated as Le Coudret was simple and fresh.

Despite its lavishness, the house in Boulevard Jules Sandeau had the distinct Dior touch. Furniture of many styles was mixed together: he worked at a fine Louis XVI desk, for instance, in a Napoleonic chair decorated with two imperial eagles, and the rooms were crowded with a hotchpotch of priceless *objets d'art*, photographs, magnificent paintings and mementoes of happy days. 'Dior does not decorate in any one style,' wrote the magazine *Maison et Jardin*, but in the wealth of all the past – and the present. Each room has so many moods, so many points of view that it would take at least two or more photographs of each one to show what it is really like.' The most famous room in the house became the bathroom. It was known that Dior liked to design in his bath, and newspapers loved to recount that his bath in Paris was made of imitation marble and silver plate.

At the Boulevard Jules Sandeau, Dior employed a permanent staff of five and, twice a week, the famous florist Dedeban sent people to arrange flowers. They would move about the house in soft felt slippers so as not to scratch the floors.

'The great charm of the house,' wrote American *Vogue*, 'lies not only in the fact of immediate beauty, but in the instantly perceptible *ambiance* of a household well and happily managed, reflecting in a dozen simultaneous ways the point of view of the man who lives there.'

A few years later Dior sold Le Coudret, the mill house, for he had found the *real* place of his dreams – the château of La Colle Noire in Montauroux, only a couple of kilometres from the village of Callian where he had lived with his father and sister during the first year of the War. His father has since died but Cathérine Dior is still living happily in Callian growing scented roses for sale to the perfume industry. Dior restored the battered old house and prepared great schemes for the property. He planted vines and even designed

a label for the bottles of wine he hoped one day to produce. 'La Colle Noire is simple, ancient and dignified,' said Dior. 'I hope its dignity conveys the period of life which I am entering. I think of this house now as my real home, the home to which, God willing, I shall one day retire, the home where perhaps I will one day forget Christian Dior, couturier, and become the neglected private individual again.'

There is a touch of regret in those words and indeed, there was sadness in Dior. Although rich and successful and loved by his staff and his friends, Dior 'was by nature a melancholy man' says Madame Raymonde. Though Cathérine Dior remembers him as a bright, happy, joking child and youth, the tremendous responsibility brought by success seems to have weighed him down. He could be funny – he once told a persistently questioning fashion editor that after his next Collection women 'would be wearing legs on their shoulders' (his next Collection featured leg-of-mutton sleeves) – but he did not laugh easily, though when he did 'he'd laugh like a child, for a quarter of an hour'.

Dior was a homosexual and although he had several affairs he never found a permanent partner to share his good fortune. Perhaps his greatest delight was in the purely paternal love he felt for Yves Saint Laurent. This young designer had been recommended to Dior by Michel de Brunhoff, the Director of French *Vogue*. Dior had been greatly impressed by the shy boy's talent and decided to take him on. 'I'll never forget his arrival,' recalls Madame Raymonde. 'He was so shy and he looked so fragile with his bony body and huge glasses. And he was so solemn, *so* solemn. He never laughed.'

Yves Saint Laurent had collaborated on Dior's last Collections and it was Dior's plan to introduce him to the Press at his very next Collection in February as his co-designer and collaborator. But it was not to be.

In October 1957 Madame Raymonde and Dior set out on their pre-Collection trip. Dior's health had not been good and it was thought that a holiday at the spa town of Montecatini in Italy would do him good. They had been there for a week, following a strict diet, but it had depressed Dior and he had insisted on taking a day off to enjoy some proper food. 'That evening he seemed so very sad. I asked him what was the matter,' remembers Madame Raymonde. 'He didn't answer my question, then he said: "Raymonde, whatever happens to me I want Yves to take over." I thought it would do him good to speak to Yves on the telephone, so we rang him up and Dior talked to him.'

They went to bed that night leaving the communicating doors between their bedrooms open – Dior always felt happier that way. As she washed and prepared for bed, Madame Raymonde could hear him moving about next door, but then a sudden silence made her feel uneasy. She went in to investigate and found Dior dying: he had had a heart attack.

His body was flown back to Paris in a special aeroplane, the House of Dior was draped in black and the grief-stricken staff – including Dior's favourites, the young mannequins – went into mourning. The stunned world of fashion turned out *en masse* for his funeral. Fellow couturiers, elegant and fashionable women – such as the Duchess of Windsor – textile workers, lace makers, embroiderers, milliners, jewellers, as well as Dior's devoted staff and his many friends from all branches of the arts, came to pay homage. The coffin, draped in black, was covered with hundreds of sprigs of lily of the valley, his lucky flower. After the solemn requiem Mass said in the chapel of Saint-Honoré d'Eylau in Paris, Dior's body was taken to the South of France, to lie, as he had asked that it should, in the village cemetery of Callian, near his beloved home of La Colle Noire. And in nearby Montauroux in an old chapel which was once part of La Colle Noire estate but which Dior gave to the village, a Mass is said for Christian Dior every year and a bouquet of red roses is laid on his grave.

Dior's coffin covered with his favourite flowers, lilies of the valley.

VO*U*

Par
S
Co
Pro
Su

Dagmar

1947

THE NEW LOOK

Christian Dior's name for his first Collection was quiet and unassuming: he called it, simply, the *Corolle* line because of the flower-like way the huge skirts blossomed out from slender, stem-like waists. But no one had time to remember what Dior thought his Collection should be called because, in the middle of the unexpected hullabaloo that greeted its appearance, an American journalist nicknamed it the New Look, and as the New Look it has gone down in history.

SPRING

Vogue reported that two things were the talk of Paris that February in 1947: the cold, and Dior. (Even fashion editors are human – they put the cold first.) It was Europe's worst winter since 1870 and France, like Britain, was still suffering terribly from wartime shortages. There was little coal, electricity was rationed and Paris was buried in snow. Shivering journalists and some buyers (but not as many as had been hoped for) turned up for the couture Collections hoping for a story – and found themselves with a tale to tell for the rest of their lives: how they actually witnessed the historic première of the New Look Collection. There was, that day, according to *Vogue's* report, 'such an air of contagious confidence in the *atelier* and salons of the new house that shortages of heat, light and transportation were forgotten in pure pleasure . . .'

'Perhaps nowhere but in Paris would the rise of a new designing star cause such general excitement,' *Vogue* commented, pointing out that: 'Not limited to the couture world or the world of fashionable women,

Dior's first Collection – the cover of American *Vogue*. For this dress the hips were heavily padded under the long torso-fitting top. The skirt was pleated and full. DAGMAR.

29

the talk of the town at the moment is Dior.' Dior quickly became the subject of heated discussion not only in Paris but throughout the Western world, with government officials, politicians and taxi drivers joining in the debate along with fashion editors, designers, journalists and house-wives. (This year, 34 years since the New Look was launched, I looked on in amazement as my mother and a friend – both in their seventies – joined battle about whether the New Look had been morally right or wrong.)

To understand all the emotion that the New Look unwittingly triggered off, one needs to know how women had dressed during the long war years. Cloth and labour shortages had meant that in both Britain and America the amount of fabric and trimming that could be used in a garment was restricted. In Britain, clothes were rationed as well, and better known than any brand name was the famous Utility mark, signifying that a garment had passed the government's strict price and quality control. As a result, wartime clothes for women were austere and unfeminine, with their mannish jackets, square shoulders and short straight skirts.

Dressed in this way themselves, the Press and buyers crammed into the Dior salon to watch the unknown new boy's opening show. *Vogue's* Bettina Ballard was among them, and recalled what she felt in her memoirs: 'I was conscious of an electric tension that I had never before felt in the couture. Suddenly, all the confusion subsided, everyone was seated and there was a moment of hush that made my skin prickle. The first girl came out, stepping fast, switching with a provocative swing-ing movement, whirling in the close-packed room, knocking over ashtrays with the strong flare of her pleated skirt and bringing everyone to the edges of their seats. After a few more costumes had passed all at the same exciting tempo, the audience knew that Dior had created a new look. We were witness to a revolution in fashion . . .'

Dior's *Corolle* line, the New Look, was the exact opposite of what women had been wearing for the last seven years. Here were skirts that used up to 15 – even 25 – yards of material and reached down nearly to the ankles. (The story goes that towards the end of the show, women in the audience were self-consciously tugging at their short skirts, trying to make them cover their knees.) Waists were nipped-in and tiny, often with a shaped leather belt. Bodices were neat and close-fitting and emphasized rounded breasts. The crude square pads had gone from the shoulders, and hips were made fuller with pleats or pads instead.

Legs and feet looked adorably pretty in opera pumps with slim heels and pointed toes. Hats were tip-tilted to one side in a flirty way, and Maharajah-sized fake diamonds glittered in chokers around pale necks. Jackets had pinched-in waists too, with peplums that flared out to emphasize the hips; and even the straight skirts Dior showed were feminine and flattering and bore no resemblance to the boxy wartime kind. Pleats whirled, silks rustled, petticoats peeped and the audience became ecstatic. There were cries of *bravo!, ravissant!* and *magnifique!* through-out the show and thunderous applause at the end.

Vogue put across the message with solemnity: 'There are moments when fashion changes funda-mentally,' it announced. 'This is one of those moments. Granted that we in England will not partake of it very far or very fast at present: it is still something that has happened of which we should be aware in every purchase and every renovation.'

They were right in everything, except how quickly the New Look would catch on, for within a year it was accepted everywhere. Though war-time restrictions still applied, manufacturers could get round them by producing the New Look in limited quantities of non-Utility garments. Dereta, a British firm, took a gamble right away and made a grey flannel New Look suit: 700 of them walked out of a West End store within two weeks. Manufacturers with stock of the square wartime clothes found the market for them had disappeared. Christian Dior's clothes had made everything else seem dull and out-of-date.

Even women who could afford neither coupons nor money for a whole new outfit could add a frill or false hem to an existing skirt and cinch in the waist with a belt. In a report from Paris, *Vogue* noted: 'There is much mixing of materials – a good pointer to renovation possibilities with the over-short skirts in our present wardrobes.'

The British Board of Trade ranted and raved against the insane extravagance of the new fashion. Editors were asked to play down the new clothes and when they seemed reluctant to oblige, Sir Stafford Cripps, the Board's president, thumped the table and cried: 'There should be a law!' Bessie Braddock, the down-to-earth, north-country MP, spoke for many when she called the New Look 'the ridiculous whim of idle people... people who worry about longer skirts might do something more useful with their lives.' When Dior himself visited Chicago that year, he was met by angry women carrying placards saying 'Burn Mr Dior!' and 'Christian Dior go home!'

Reactions were a little like those which greeted the appearance of Courrèges' short skirts in 1964, but more intense: outrage and condemnation on one side and applause and acceptance on the other, from those who understood that this was not an entirely frivolous business but the reflection of a genuine change of mood in society, a fashion that fulfilled a real yearning.

The New Look was a shot in the arm and nothing could stop it. Dior himself said that it became symbolic of youth and hope and the future. And so it did, in spite of the fact that in many ways his dresses actually harked back to the past, to Victorian and Edwardian times – in the way they were constructed, for instance.

Dior's dresses may have looked more curvy and natural than the austere wartime ones, but what went on underneath to produce that effect became a legend in itself. A Dior dress had so much scaffolding inside that it could almost stand up alone. The fabric of each one was lined with tulle and that in turn was lined with fine silk to prevent it scratching or laddering stockings. There was padding and pleating to shape all the skirts out over hips, and bodices over busts. There were special boned corsets made of black tulle for each dress to cinch in the waist and push up the breasts: sometimes these were frilled on hip and bra cup to achieve an even more curvy shape. Evening dresses had the corsets built in so that the wearer had only to step in, naked, and the dress did the rest.

But war-weary women did not seem to mind going backwards in fashion. On the contrary, they grasped with both hands the chance to look pretty and pampered again, to bathe in nostalgia for the good old days, to have a last fling at unashamed femininity. As Dior said simply: 'I brought back the neglected art of pleasing.'

AUTUMN
Dior's second Collection, shown in July 1947, was the New Look again 'pushed to extremes,' he said. Dresses were even longer and skirts took up even more material. 'A Golden Age seemed to have come again,' Dior recalled in his memoirs. 'War had passed out of sight and there were no others on the horizon. What did the weight of my sumptuous materials, my heavy velvets and brocades matter? When hearts were light, mere fabrics could not weigh the body down.'

The New Look needed a New Look in underwear. The special corset went underneath some of the dresses – the hourglass shape accentuated by frills. 'Without foundations there can be no fashion,' said Dior. COFFIN.

31

Dior's suit, *far right*, was made of black wool and 'Paris loves it' exclaimed American *Vogue*. The fitted jacket belled out over padding and the full skirt emphasized the feminine line. The gloves, slender umbrella and opera pumps completed the elegant look. BALKIN.

The pale tussore silk jacket, *centre*, was also padded over the hips, like a tea cosy. It was the best selling suit from Dior's New Look Collection and yards and yards of fabric went into the black, knife-pleated skirt. BALKIN.

Both the jacket and skirt of the suit, *right*, had knife pleats, adding fullness at the back. ERIC.

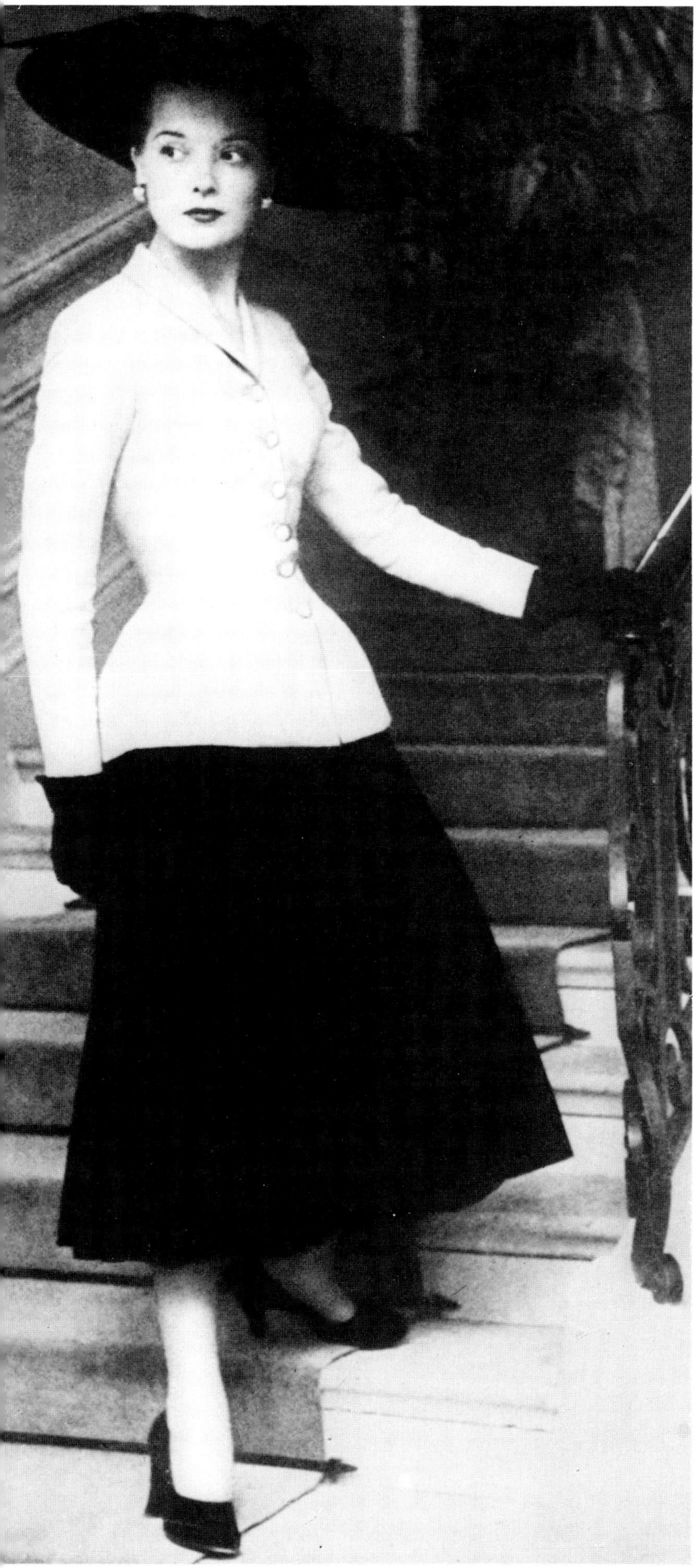

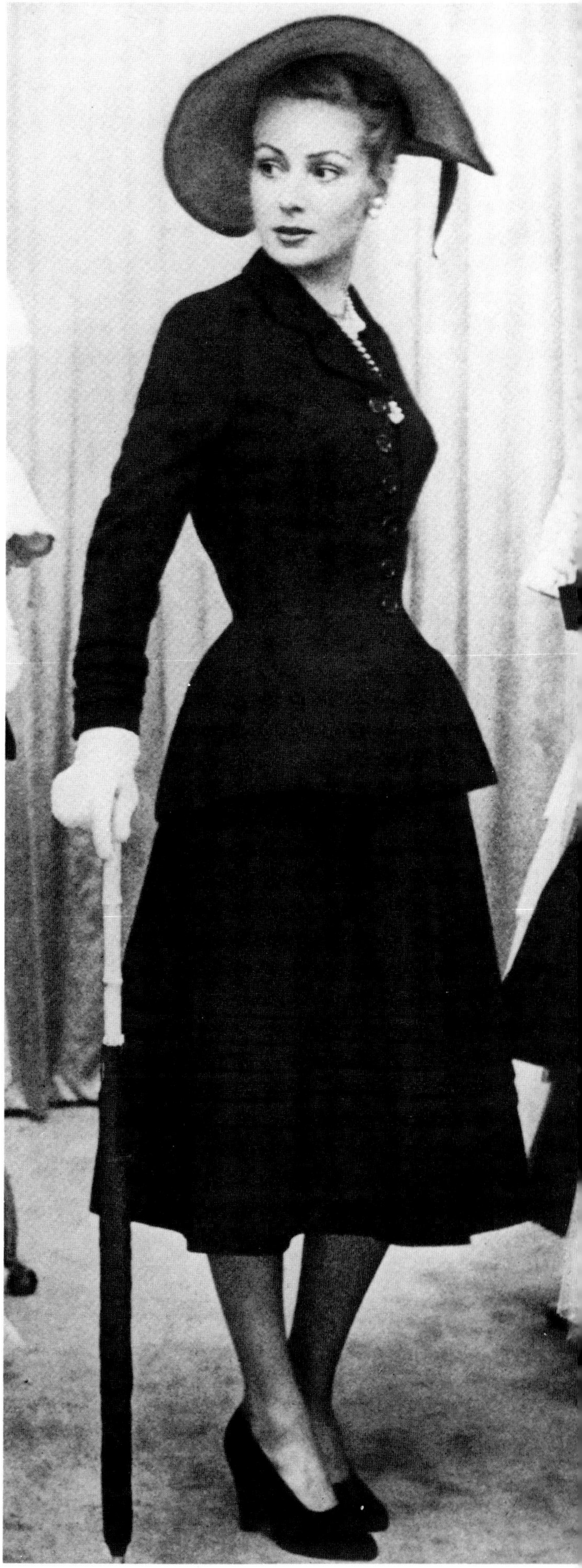

The Gibson Girl blouse in beige silk, *above*, teamed with a full skirt took on the New Look style. BALKIN.

D ior's taffeta dinner dress, *above*,
was made of 25 yards of material.
'Your own shoulders,' said *Vogue*, 'plus padded hips.' BALKIN.

African sun hat and pleated pongee dress, *below*. BALKIN. The silk surah day dress, *right*, had a scarf drapery at the back of the full skirt. BALKIN. Neck-to-hem, back-buttoned grey linen dress, *far right*. The hips were gently rounded and the waist was emphasized by a belt. BALKIN.

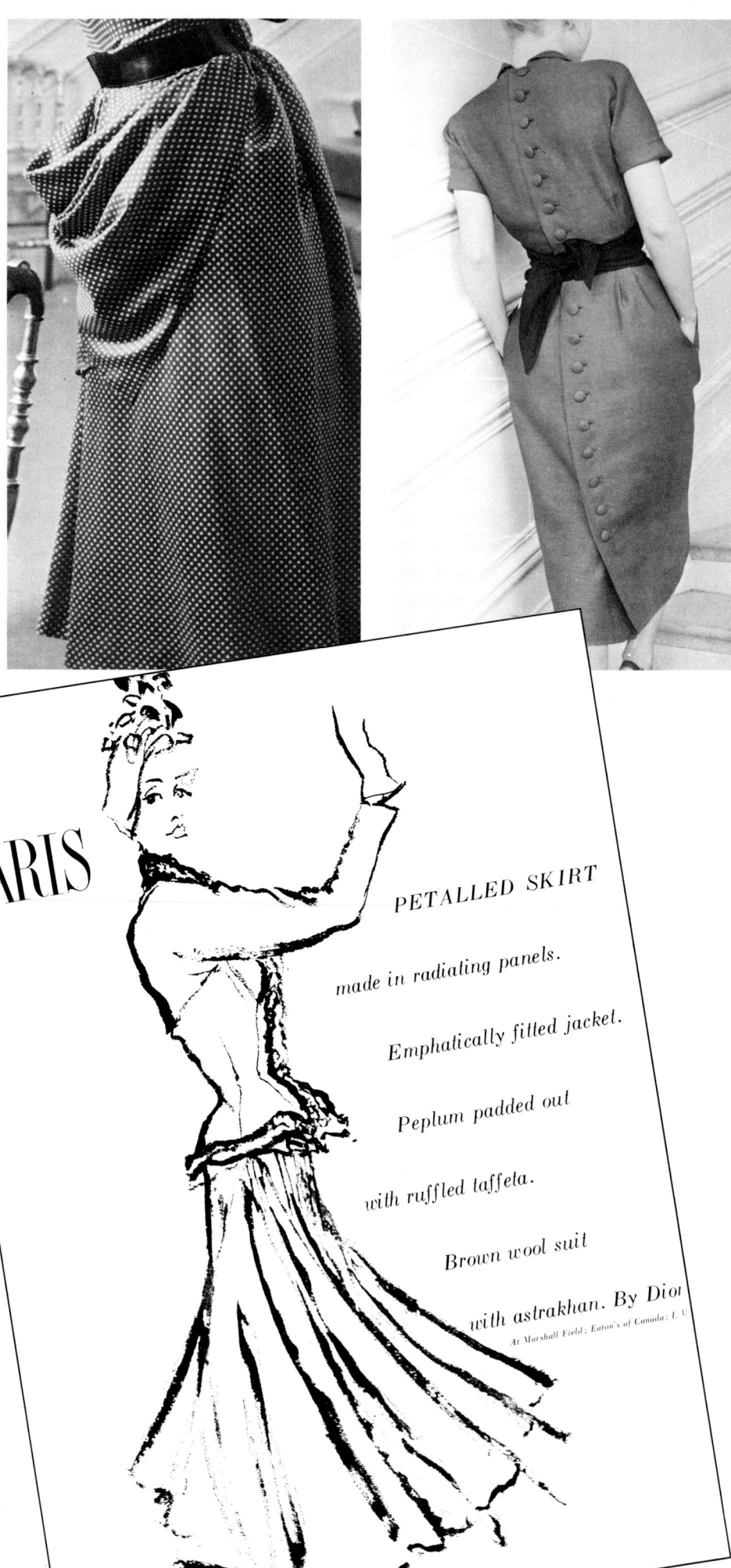

PARIS

PETALLED SKIRT

made in radiating panels.

Emphatically fitted jacket.

Peplum padded out

with ruffled taffeta.

Brown wool suit

with astrakhan. By Dior

At Marshall Field; Eaton's of Canada; I. M.

The grey suit, *left*, had a close-fitting belted jacket. over a long box-pleated skirt. BALKIN. The full-skirted dress, *far left*, flared into many accordion pleats, both in the skirt and on the bust. BALKIN.

SHELFED JACKET

Propped-up peplum over

blade skirt. Small shoulders

grow to puffed-out sleeves.

By Dior. At L. Hudson's

Side hat, tied on. Maud Roser.

The black-lined, beige gabardine jacket, *above*, had elbow-length sleeves and a tie back. BALKIN. Natural shoulders were the main attraction of the check suit, *top*. The jacket was closely curved to the body and matched a barrel skirt. BALKIN.

The typical Dior New Look dress, *opposite*, was nipped in at the waist and padded above and below. It had the lowest neckline in Paris and his favourite tip-tilted hat. BLUMENFELD.

Fifteen yards of material went into the skirt of the New Look cocktail dress, *above left*, with its neat bodice, belt, jewelled choker and flirty hat. BLUMENFELD.

Utterly feminine; Dior's cocktail dress, *below left*, named Maxim, had a low *décolletage*, fine waist, puffed out skirt and a bow at the bodice. Worn with a cartwheel hat. BALKIN.

The black coat, *below*, with fur collar, keeps to the New Look outline of tiny waist, full skirt and hat worn on the side of the head. BLUMENFELD.

Dior's New Look coats had the tiny waists and full skirts of the dresses. This one, *opposite*, was worn over a dress of black, pleated taffeta. ERIC.

The tiny figure-hugging bodice of the dress, *above*, is typical of the New Look Collection. So is the hat worn right on the side of the head and the beaded choker. HORST. The peplums of Dior's New Look suits, *top*, were padded – even over tight skirts – to emphasize the hips. HORST.

1948

ENVOL AND ZIG-ZAG

In 1948 *Vogue* reported that: 'The Autumn Paris Collections had the largest American audience since 1939.' But there were no real fashion fireworks that year, and 1948 owed its crowds to 1947. Dior's New Look Collection had done more than make him famous, it had also re-established Paris as the hub of the fashion world. Before the New Look was shown, there had been distinct rumblings in the clothing industries of both Britain and America – rumblings of independence, almost mutiny. During the war years they had managed to produce clothes without looking towards Paris – why should they not continue alone? When Dior sent an emissary to New York to announce the opening of the new Maison Christian Dior and drum up custom among the powerful American buyers, she was often rebuffed. 'We have our own designers now,' she was told, 'why should we go to Paris?' She wrote back to Monsieur Dior: 'I am not at all sure they will come.'

In fact, there were only 18 American buyers at the first showing of the New Look, but dozens more journeyed to Paris to catch up on what they had missed once the news of the New Look had broken. Within weeks, Dior had to demolish an old staircase and enlarge the landing outside his salons in order to accommodate the crowds. Even then, there was not enough room, and the overspill of guests had to perch on the main staircase – in strict order of precedence of course, rather like exotic birds very conscious of their pecking order. From then on, the power and prestige of Christian Dior attracted up to 25,000 visitors to his Collections each season. Journalists came to report on them for the newly fashion-conscious public; buyers

D ior's dramatic *Envol* skirt was caught up at the back and stiffened to jut out over its underskirt. COFFIN.

came from all over the world to choose the most commercial of the models for copying or adapting, and women who were rich enough came to buy their own clothes.

In 1948, *Vogue* claimed that the Paris Collections helped to account for the sudden growth of traffic across the Atlantic – 250,000 people crossed from America to Europe that summer. Among them were 'American women: private clients of French makers before the War, younger ones who had never seen a Paris Collection before. They came in numbers, crowded into the couture houses, placed their orders ... And the American manufacturers, the fashion directors of the great and small shops, came, looked and bought ... As a consequence,' *Vogue* added practically, 'most of the things you see in this issue are, or will be, in American shops.'

SPRING
That spring, the Collection itself offered no real surprises. The New Look of the previous year had utterly changed the way women looked, and it was to remain a basic shape for some time. Even Dior could not spring a New Look on the public every year: instead, he concentrated on developing his original idea and adding brilliant touches to make it sparkle again. He named this Collection *Envol*, meaning 'Flight', or 'Winged', but it was really the New Look given a bit of extra oomph. In the more flowery words of Monsieur Dior himself: 'the silhouette achieved its peak of youth and flightiness.'

Skirts, still long of course, were given lots of movement by scooping them up at one side or, bustle-like, at the back, or simply by pushing all the fullness towards what *Vogue* coyly called the 'derrière'. The new, short jacket with its loose, fly-away back proved to be popular, as did the introduction of dramatic, stand-up collars. Giant cuffs, added to some jackets, were described by *Vogue* as 'flapping like seal fins'.

AUTUMN
Zig-zag was the name given to the Autumn Collection, its aim being to 'give the figure the animated look of a drawing'. Its hallmarks were the curious asymmetrical – or, if you like, zig-zag – necklines given to evening dresses. There were

one-shoulder dresses, one-sleeve dresses and a complicated system of draping and wrapping bodices to produce a neckline that went off at a tangent. A much simpler idea was the introduction of long, tight sleeves on cocktail and dinner dresses. Skirts were given uneven, zig-zag hemlines to make them fit in to the zig-zag theme.

By now, Dior's accessories were as influential as his clothes. This year, he decreed ropes of pearls twined around the neck, umbrellas and gloves, swathed cummerbunds and wide leather belts; scarves were worn knotted in big bows under suit collars; shoes had fabric trimmings or gaiters in material to match the main outfit.

Vogue summed it all up after the Autumn shows: 'Most of the Collection news is detail. A skirt-length, a cuff, a neckline is suddenly more important than any one silhouette.' Perhaps some of those present felt that this was an anticlimax after the excitement of the year before, but mostly, *Vogue* reported, audiences were 'wholly relieved' that the Collections were 'a continuation of, not a departure from, silhouette lines already established.'

Vogue called the dress, *opposite*, 'the loveliest new summer look'; pale pink chiffon with a New Look skirt. NEPO. The long sleeves, *above*, on the New Look black *faille* dinner dress were a 1948 touch. NEPO.

Typical of the Collection:
the high-collared fly-
away jacket in black wool,
right, worn over a pencil slim
dress. The umbrella and gloves
were important to the overall
look. KEOGH.

A pencil slim black wool
dress, *below*, topped by
a short jacket with fly-away
back, high collar and giant
cuffs. Other new touches:
gaiters and a giant pussy cat
bow at the neck. COFFIN.

The black wool dress, *above*, had the figure-hugging bodice of the New Look but the dramatic caught-up skirt and the winged hat were intended to emphasize the *Envol* (or Winged) theme. NEPO.

Dior's tiered coat, *left*, in his favourite black and white checks. The cape top emphasized the soft sloping shoulders. NEPO.

Vogue called this 'the great suit' of Dior's Zig-Zag Collection for the autumn 1948, *left*. The zig-zag angular peplum was stiffened, the skirt fullness all at the back. Note the gauntlet-style gloves. COFFIN.

Dior's dramatic new zig-zag collar, *above*, jutting backwards on this grey flannel, back-buttoning dress. *Vogue* called this outfit a 'Ford', meaning that it would probably sell as well as the motor car of that name. The buttons down the back and emphasizing the hip pockets were a favourite Dior touch and a haberdasher's dream come true. The neat cloche hat was popular in 1948. COFFIN.

Dior continued the soft-
shouldered cape theme,
in this coat, *right*. The cape back
melted into the sleeves. DACQUEAU.
The day dress, *above*, with one
shoulder draping, wide
cummerbund and handkerchief
trailing from the pocket,
emphasized the asymmetry of the
Zig-Zag Collection. COFFIN.

In the autumn of
1948 Dior so loved
zig-zags and asymmetry
that he designed skirts
wrapped onto one hip,
gently exposing the leg.
The black wool dress, *left*,
'changes the look of after-
dark fashion', said *Vogue*.
The large hat was in black
velvet. ERIC.

51

Dior's gala dresses were unbeatable for glamour and grandeur. The dress, *right*, in yards and yards of white tulle had a strapless bodice and was worn under a duster coat of blue satin, trimmed with gold lace. COFFIN.

Asymmetry appeared again in the pearl grey satin evening dress, *above*, with a draped and wrapped neckline and a single sleeve. COFFIN.

1949

TROMPE L'OEIL AND MID-CENTURY

In a Gallup Poll taken in 1949, Christian Dior was rated the fifth best-known man in the world. By now his daily postbag bulged with letters from as far afield as Australia, America and Japan, most of them from grateful women: 'You waved your wand and suddenly I was young and hopeful again. I love you.' But there was hate mail too: 'My wife looks like a stuffed doll . . . I shall tear you apart on my next visit to Paris,' or, 'With your so-called genius you have succeeded in disfiguring my wife . . . what would you say if I sent you the remains?'

SPRING

Dior was not afraid of putting pen to paper himself. He was the first couturier to christen his Collections, to give each new line a name – A line, H line and so on, and every season he would carefully compose a press release for distribution at the opening show outlining his current fashion philosophy, so that journalists would understand what they were looking at. Dior's explanation of his *Trompe l'oeil* Collection took up four pages, although in essence what it amounted to was a line that emphasized the width of the bust and gave the skirts lots of movement without adding any bulk.

In this appropriately named Collection, Dior used all sorts of tricks to make busts look wider: huge revers jutted out on either side like wings, giant collars over-lapped the shoulders, pockets were placed high on the bodice or on the bust itself. But for evening there was a much more straightforward way of emphasizing the

This sexy black dress epitomized the new worldly look for after dark. In silk surah it had a revealingly spiral skirt and an off-the-shoulder neckline. RUTLEDGE.

bosom – Dior simply made his dresses barer and barer. There were wide sweeping *décolletés*, daring plunge necklines and lots of strapless dresses. (As a child, a treat I looked forward to was being allowed to powder my older sister's back and shoulders when she wore her daring strapless Dior-copy dress.)

To achieve the important feeling of movement without heaviness or bulk, he put flying panels or pleats on nearly every skirt; when standing still the figure looked slender and lean, but with movement the panels fluttered and flew.

Dior's hats became particularly popular this season. There were all manner of side-swooping hats, dramatic bicorne hats and his favourite cartwheel hats, but by far the most successful was his dear little 'imp' hat with a zig-zag edge – it was copied again and again.

It was a clever Collection, with enough of the previous year's *Envol* and Zig-zag lines to make it make sense plus masses of new ideas, and Dior also provided a quick glimpse into the future with some bloused dresses and suits. *Vogue* approved, commenting that women's bodies had been 'neither betrayed nor deformed'.

AUTUMN

Dior's Autumn Collection was called the Mid-century look, for although it was shown in July to the Press and buyers, the clothes were to be worn in the winter of 1949 to 1950. *Vogue* was enthusiastic about it: 'As he did in his first triumphant Collection, he has seized on the beginnings of a change in fashion, dramatized it, lifted it to magnificent beauty.'

The new Dior dresses and suits were softly bloused on top with tiny belted waists and pencil skirts so narrow they clearly needed the famous 'Dior Pleat' (a slit backed with a panel of fabric) so that the girls could walk. There were dresses with full skirts too, but these were flowing and easy, and not the padded crinolines of the New Look.

That season's bloused and belted jackets and bodices were very different to the neat-fitting New Look ones, but the look was easy and full of vitality. *Vogue* said his dresses looked like 'first cousins' to the American shirtwaister. Evening dresses were slick and sexy and very worldly;

they were usually short, often strapless and nearly always pencil slim. Dior invented a new skirt for them – the Scissor skirt – which had two 'blades' of fabric over a slender underskirt.

Hats seemed to defy the laws of nature, and were plastered to the side of the head. Sleeves were often three-quarter length, which meant, in the dramatic words of French *Vogue*, that 'the reign of the glove has begun'; gloves and umbrellas were now 'indispensable accessories'. (Indeed I can never think of those tight pencil skirts without imagining an umbrella in the picture – perhaps the girls needed them to keep their balance in those exaggerated poses.) Other favourite accessories were handkerchiefs tucked into pockets and buttonholes of flowers. Dior was a hopelessly superstitious man and never showed a Collection without including somewhere a posy of his lucky flower, lily of the valley. This year they were to be seen popping out of one of his big new pockets.

Once again, Dior had produced a masterful mixture of the most feminine clothes imaginable, or, as *Vogue* described them, 'beautifully designed, desirable clothes with the fixed purpose of interesting, of dramatizing a woman.'

In his *Trompe l'Oeil* Collection Dior used all sorts of tricks to get this message across. In particular there were flying panels or pleated panels on almost every garment to give the feeling of movement and width without bulk. This black wool dress sums up the look with its sinuous shape and flying back panel. The bust was made to look rounder by pockets on the bodice. RUTLEDGE.

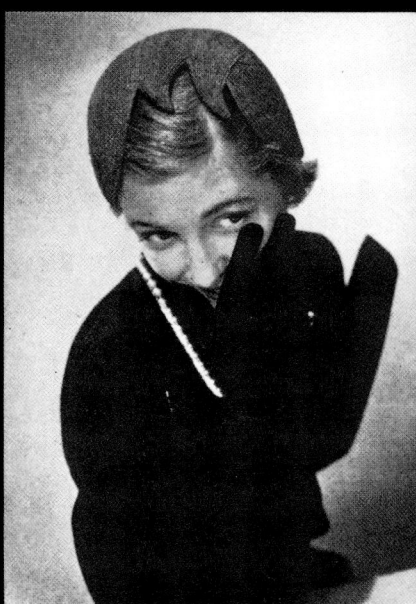

Dior's winning hat, in the spring 1949, was the little imp hat, *above*, in red with its edge cut in points. NEPO.

The beige linen-look dress, *below left*, from the Spring Collection, had a sweeping double collar to give the bodice breadth. The skirt had Dior's favourite button-trimmed pockets and the new hat shape was a dramatic bicorne. NEPO.
One's eye could hardly miss the bust on the dress, *above left*, with its cross-over pearls and extraordinary winged protuberances. NEPO.
A swinging pleated panel on the skirt, *centre*, features Dior's new pocket, stiffened to stand away from the body. RUTLEDGE.

Dior's bloused look was the success of autumn 1949. This suit, *right*, summed it up: dropped shoulders and flounced sleeves (lined in beaver) to emphasize width, bodice bloused above a tiny belted waist, a pencil slim skirt. BOUCHÉ.

The grey flannel dress, *far right*, called Mère Michèle, had a bloused bodice, belted waist, a flounced skirt and sleeves, and dropped shoulders. It was worn with an arrow hat. BOUCHÉ.

Vogue called the easy
bloused dress, *below*, 'first
cousin to the American
shirtwaister'. The jet-beaded hat
had a fluttering veil. 'To him the
accessory is always a part, not
apart,' punned *Vogue*. HORST.
Proving the point was the grey
suit, *right*, with beige gloves,
alligator handbag and wool scarf,
crossed and tucked into the
belt. MCLAUGHLIN.

Dior's new parka-jacket, *above*, bloused and belted with a hood. The model had the new, short urchin haircut. HORST.

Dior added giant, sloping epaulettes to emphasize the width of the bloused and belted jacket, *left*, in hairy tweed. HORST.

The short, bare evening dress, *left.* Dior's strapless, black wool dress had a panel of moiré silk buttoned onto the hips and sweeping down to the floor. BOUCHÉ

The new scissor skirts for Dior's pencil-slim, strapless evening dresses, *right,* were made of 'blades' of satin or velvet over narrow, black broadcloth skirts. Note the short, boyish haircut and flirty face veil. HORST.

1950

VERTICAL AND OBLIQUE LINE

What makes fashion? Dior was asked over and over again. He always replied that there were four main ingredients: 'a certain feeling in the air' was the first, and perhaps the most important. That feeling, he explained, could be caused 'by the success of a play, the impact of a society ball, one woman's elegance, a political event, an exhibition, the state visit of a sovereign'. Logic and luck were the next two ingredients and the last was purely practical – what the magazines chose to promote. But, Dior insisted, it was women themselves who were the ultimate arbiters of fashion: 'The couturier proposes, but woman herself disposes,' he said.

Cynics had suggested that Dior created the New Look with its hugely full skirts to please Monsieur Boussac, who was in the business of selling cotton – a suggestion that made Dior furious. 'I swear that any fashion inspired by that sort of consideration would have no chance of surviving, still less of succeeding and developing.'

SPRING

In spring 1950 Dior launched the straight, up-and-down look which he called the Vertical line. With this look, the quantity of fabric used in each outfit was reduced but, since many of the garments were made entirely in tucked or pleated cloths, the fabric manufacturers greeted it with more enthusiasm than they had shown for his pencil skirts.

The Vertical line was not one of Dior's historic Collections, but nevertheless it was packed with ideas and was widely copied. Vertical line clothes were for spring

A glittering oval jewel often appeared in Dior's Autumn Collection 1950. Sometimes it was pinned on one shoulder, sometimes to one glove. PENN.

The essence of Dior's Vertical line for spring 1950, *far right*. A straight up-and-down narrow dress in pleated chiffon. There are no sleeves or collar to interrupt the line. ERIC. Dior elongated many collars; the most popular was the horseshoe collar on the boxy jacket, *right*. ERIC.

and summer, and, logically, dresses were more often sleeveless – 'helping to create the look of a straight line between shoulder and hip that Dior was aiming at. French *Vogue* did a whole page on How to Beautify Arms, which it described (somewhat hysterically) as being 'naked as a silver dish, naked as a church wall'.

Bare arms had been perfectly acceptable for the beach or for evening, but now, 'apart from certain dresses for lunch, the races, tea and garden parties, arms will be thus: completely revealed from the shoulder ...' French *Vogue* would never have believed that in less than 20 years some women would be seen 'topless' – but that is another story. In the meantime it recommended gymnastics, creams, tinted foundation creams and scents to help keep arms in perfect shape.

Dior's Vertical line also meant new, straight boxy jackets in all lengths, and loose duster coats. He invented two new collar shapes to emphasize the Vertical line: enormously long revers that plunged down almost to the waist, or a curved version of the same thing that was known as the horseshoe collar, and was widely copied.

AUTUMN
Dior stayed with geometry for his Autumn Collection, which he named the Oblique line. There were reappearances of the asymmetrical necklines and bodices he had loved in previous seasons: clothes were wrapped to the side or fastened on one side, necklines slanted sideways, tucks and seams spiralled around the body. He described the complicated cutting and stitching involved as 'work done by fairy fingers, which characterizes Paris couture', and it is true that many of these clothes could not be copied cheaply.

Vogue especially liked the new Dior accessories: a gauntlet glove with a cuff so deep it could contain a purse; a huge, glittering brooch worn on a shoulder, a cuff, on the hair, or attached to one ear only (giving an Oblique look to earrings); and the Dior mannequins' new hairstyle – a tiny, twisted chignon on the top of the head.

Skirt lengths were no surprise in 1950. They had been creeping up to mid-calf length ever since the two first Collections, and were now about 14 inches from the ground (in heels, of course).

Dior's new horseshoe collar is featured, *right*, on a New Look-type suit with a nipped-in waist and pencil skirt. ERIC.

Dior's Oblique line meant everything
slanted to one side. The short, black
crêpe evening dress, *above*, had diagonal tucks and
the gloves were cut to slant across the upper arm
and shoulders – unbelievably, these buttoned
at the back. A giant, glittering jewel was fastened
to the tulle headdress – to one side, of course.
PENN.

Whatever the major theme of a
Collection, a Dior show always
included an extravagant gala evening dress with
crinoline skirts. This one, *left*, in layers of pleated
tulle, was fashionably bare. PARKINSON.

Dior's new tunic-length jackets were tightly belted and – to emphasize the Oblique line – fastened to one side. A typical touch was the giant fur muff, *right*. PENN.

To achieve the Oblique look Dior invented a new, built-in scarf at the neck, *opposite left*, which wrapped firmly across the body and tucked into the belt at one side. It worked perfectly on this neat grey wool suit. PENN.

Τhe tunic-length jacket, *above*, was successful. It buttoned to one side and slanted into a tightly waisted belt. The pencil skirt and handkerchief peeping from the sleeve complemented the outfit. PENN.

The new Oblique collar slanted out to a jutting point on the belted coat, *left*, with padded hips and deep armholes. PENN. In autumn 1950 Dior's mannequins wore their hair twisted into chignons, high on the head, *above*. PENN.

A black wool dress, *right*, from the Oblique Collection. Softly feminine with a flirty skirt, pearls and a peeping handkerchief. PENN.

1951

OVAL AND LONG LINE

Fashion nowadays is so little concerned with dress-making – the art of shaping and manipulating cloth by means of seams and darts, draping and cutting – and so much involved with the overall 'look' instead, that it is astonishing to realize how much detail mattered 30 years ago.

In March 1951, for instance, *Vogue* boasted 116 sketches from the Paris Collection – sketches of new cuffs, new collars, new skirts, new necklines and new shoulders. 'In the decisive hours of a change of season,' it said ponderously, 'the duty of *Vogue* is not only to present the creations of our great designers in an agreeable way, but to explain clearly the new tendencies in fashion.'

But of course, couture houses were different then too. In charge of Dior's work-rooms was the fabled Madame Marguerite, whose job it was to interpret his sketches into cloth. Dior used to congratulate her on having a 'sculptor's thumb', for Madame Marguerite and her staff could literally mould fabrics with a hot iron to fit the contours of the human body. 'Shaping materials like this is something ready-to-wear could not do,' she explained. 'They put in darts instead.'

SPRING

The Oval line that Dior launched in the spring of 1951 was a masterpiece of dressmaking, Madame Marguerite's technical wizardry at its best. There were no gimmicks, just superbly constructed, flattering, womanly clothes. Every edge was rounded: suits hugged the body closely; shoulders simply smoothed into sleeves without a break, and hips and breasts were gently moulded.

The Princesse line, autumn 1951. The black wool dress was waisted just under the bust. Over it a cropped bolero jacket knotted in front. CLARKE.

Sleeves seemed to be carved out of cloth and curved at the top; collars were hardly noticeable any more – in fact, Dior often used a simple mandarin neck-band – and jackets were rounded off at the front.

His most popular hat shape, worn low over the eyes, was what *Vogue* dubbed his 'Chinese coolie' hat, but it is doubtful whether any Chinese coolie would have recognized it as such.

Perhaps it was because these clothes were so feminine that Dior felt no need to bare his ladies for evening. The sexy little dresses of past seasons gave way to elegant dinner suits in his favourite colour combination of black and white. *Vogue* loved the show and called it 'Dior's best since his first sensation'. As always in a Dior Collection, there were hints of the future as well as echoes of past shows. That spring, he introduced a new, snug bolero jacket that was so short it stopped just below the bust. It was to become the big news for autumn.

AUTUMN

Dior used to say that, of all the clothes he had ever designed, those he created for autumn 1951 were the ones he loved best. He called that Collection the Long line, but like the *Corolle* Collection, which almost immediately became known as the New Look, the Long line was soon christened the Princesse line – and that is how it will always be remembered.

Suddenly the big question of the day was, 'Where is the waistline?' *Vogue* reassured its readers: 'You are the public, you will decide. New lines are not imposed on you, you accept them because you like them or reject them because you don't.' From this solemn statement one might think that Dior had done something extraordinary: in fact, for the Princesse line, the waist actually stayed where it was, but was not emphasized by a belt. Instead, the illusion of a high waist was given by marking another line just below the bust. This was done by putting short bolero jackets, in contrasting fabrics or colours, over dresses, or by placing a seam under the bust from which gathers rose over the bosom, or by attaching a half-belt high up across the back of a jacket or coat. From this new high line, the rest of the garment, full or slim, swept down in an unbroken line to the hem. Skirts were fractionally longer to emphasize this long line; they were now 13 to 14 inches from the floor, but looked longer still because of the illusion of a higher waist.

Princesse line copies were rushed into the shops by autumn (the Collection had been shown in July) and the public decided – as *Vogue* had told them they should – in favour of Dior's Princesse line. But the saga of the wandering waist was by no means over.

The 'Chinese coolie' hat, *above*, was a hit of the Spring Collection. Worn very low over the eyes and trimmed with buttons or bows. NEPO.

Dior's ultra feminine suit, from the Oval Collection for spring 1951, *opposite*. The jacket was cut on the cross to hug the figure, the raglan sleeves ensured a smooth, curved shoulder. In grey worsted with a natural shantung blouse that showed at the neck. Dior knotted a long fur scarf on the upper arm. RAWLINGS.

87

Box jackets of the Vertical line became the barrel jackets of the Oval line in spring 1951. The one *below* had the new raglan sleeves and curved shoulder line and went over a collarless, figure-hugging suit that rounded and emphasized both hips and bust. In black and white tweed trimmed with black grosgrain and boot buttons. RAWLINGS.

These three marvellously feminine dresses, *right*, were draped to give an extra-rounded look to the hips and bodice. All were in silk printed with a pattern of butterfly wings (by Brossin de Méré). NEPO.

Dior often used a simple
Chinese mandarin collar
in spring 1951. *Right*, on a black
satin evening suit with an edge of
white appearing at the cuffs and
front fastenings. RAWLINGS.

The snugly fitting jacket,
opposite, cropped off just
below the bust, came from the
Oval line Spring Collection – note
the rounded shoulders. It was the
first glimpse of the Princesse line
that Dior was to launch in the
Autumn Collection. The jacket
was in natural shantung and the
dress in grey wool. RAWLINGS.

The grey flannel dress, *below left*, from Dior's Princesse line Collection autumn 1951, had a tiny cropped bolero jacket, to give, once again, the illusion of a high waist. The grey broadtail fur coat had a high back belt to continue the theme. CLARKE.

Vogue called the dress, *above right*, a 'simple, significant dress'. In black wool, it flowed from the neck to the hem in an unbroken, curving line with no extra emphasis at the waist. CLARKE.

Dior gave coats and jackets his new Princesse line by belting them high at the back and making all the fullness spring from that line. *Vogue* commented of the grey flannel jacket, *below right*: 'the waist is under the armpits'. CLARKE.
Above left, a navy blue coat with the new high-slung back belt. CLARKE.

Dior's elegant new evening suits, *above*, were in his favourite colour combination of black and white. *Left:* a white chiffon dress with a tight-fitting cardigan jacket of black silk. *Right:* a black satin jacket over a crêpe bodice and long, narrow, black skirt. The black gloves are long enough to meet the short puffed sleeves of the jacket. NEPO.

Dior draped and folded the bodice to make a high waist on the black wool dress, *above*. From the Princesse line Collection, autumn 1951. CLARKE.

A copy of the Princesse line, *above right*, by the British firm, Marcus. The cropped bolero jacket was in black velvet. The long-sleeved *faille* dress had a bell skirt held out on petticoats. The outfit sold for 29½ guineas. CLARKE.

Even the gala evening dress, *opposite*, acquired the new high-waisted look – a giant bow trimmed the bust, and the embroidered moons decreased in size as they rose towards the bodice. CLARKE.

1952

SINUOUS AND PROFILE LINE

By 1952 things were going better than ever at the Maison Christian Dior. Since opening day in 1947 the company had been continually forced to expand and now Dior was ruler of a substantial empire. In the mews behind his original little couture house in Avenue Montaigne, two giant, nine-storey blocks had gone up; and around the corner in Rue François Premier, vast rented buildings now housed the Dior administration. The company that had started with three workrooms employing 60 people now occupied five buildings, had 28 workrooms and over 1,000 employees. No wonder Dior occasionally felt a little trapped. 'The peaceful little business which I had envisaged is in the process of devouring me,' he said sadly.

Dior felt troubled too by events in the world outside his empire: the Iron Curtain had descended in Europe, a new war had started in Korea and there was trouble in Indochina. The heady feelings of confidence and hope for the future that had surged up after the War – and carried the New Look along in their wake – had vanished. It is easy to mock those working at the luxury end of a luxury trade for displays of feeling – I remember how we smiled when Yves Saint Laurent, years ago, put headbands across his models' foreheads to show that they were in mourning for Vietnam – but what was he to do?

In 1952 Dior's way was to edit out of his Collections what he called 'fashion fripperies', and instead he produced two of his most disciplined and sober Collections: 'The new essential of fashion is that it should be discreet,' he said.

Spring ease and effortlessness
hallmarked the Sinuous line.
Here, a marvellously simple white crêpe
dress with a pleated wrap-around bodice and
skirt. Worn under a mink coat. CLARKE.

SPRING

For spring 1952 he launched what he called the Sinuous line: soft, fluid clothes that moved with the body, made no exaggerations and looked timeless and effortless. Of all Dior's Collections, the Sinuous line looks the most modern now. The sweater dress was his main innovation: *Vogue* called it 'Dior's theme song,' adding, 'Soon, we believe, all America's.' The sweater look consisted of a three-piece outfit: a soft cardigan jacket, a simple little top (sometimes worn *outside* the skirt to give more of a sweater feeling) and a gentle skirt. Dior produced these in all kinds of fabrics but most successfully in soft crêpe and in pastel colours.

The saga of the waistline was not forgotten, however, and Dior remained loyal to his high waist, showing softer versions of his Princesse dresses and boleros. Even his new hats were soft – there was a new scarf hat that tied in a bow at the back, which became immensely popular.

AUTUMN

The casual look of the Sinuous line was a tremendous success, but while other designers took it up for autumn, Dior changed his tune and presented the Profile line. As its name suggests, this line was sharper and more defined: there were still no 'fashion fripperies' and, in fact, the clothes were simpler than ever – stark, even – and cut to outline the body in a dramatic way. Dior's favourite colour was uncompromising too: 'Black, Black, BLACK' *Vogue* told its readers, and he invented a striking new skirt, cunningly constructed to jut out over the hips.

Hats were neat: pillboxes, close-fitting turbans, tiny cones to pop on the back of the head. Skirts were a little longer – about $11\frac{1}{2}$ inches from the ground – and *Vogue* helpfully suggested that readers could use the height of the magazine as their measure. The hottest news for evening wear, that season, was the little black dress.

The sweater dress was 'Dior's theme song for spring 1952,' said *Vogue*. The dresses, *right*, were in fact soft two-pieces with cardigan jackets. HORST. Dior softened the Princesse line for spring. The bolero jacket, *opposite*, topped an ivory silk shirt. HORST.

Dior's easy duster coat, *opposite*,
had slits to the thighs and
was made of paisely-printed silk. RANDALL.

A high-waisted look for the
three-piece cocktail costume,
below left. The skirt was in black taffeta with
pleats from above the knee, the bodice in
pink with a high tucked midriff. The black
jacket was a simple wrap-around. The oval
pillbox hat with a flower was very popular.
HORST.
The Sinuous line was all softness, typified
by the pretty chiffon dress printed with
rosebuds, *below right*. The draped bodice was
strapless with the briefest tie-on jacket over it.
HORST.

1952
AUTUMN

VOGUE

WINTER PRIMER
WHAT TO WEAR WITH WHAT
WHAT TO WEAR
FOR EVENINGS OUT
HOW TO CHOOSE A FUR
HOW TO BUDGET:
UNDER £60 FOR 6 MONTHS

OCTOBER 1952
PRICE 3'6

Dior's new Profile line for autumn 1952. Stark and sober with no 'fashion fripperies', it sharply outlined the body for impact. This black jersey dress, *far right*, had a high side fastening and new skirt shape to exaggerate the hips. Dior rather humorously called it 'The Ant'. MCLAUGHLIN.

Coats followed a similar line. They too hugged the body and outlined the curves. The coat, *right*, was typically in black wool. MCLAUGHLIN.
Dior's new cone hats hugged the head as his dresses clung to the body, *above*. The 'doe eye' make-up, so popular in the Fifties was very unsophisticated by modern standards – just a line drawn up at the end of the eyes to make them look slanted, and exaggeratedly arched eyebrows. PRIGENT.

94

A fine black wool dress, *below*, that moulded to the body. Only a touch of white at the neck and a double line of buttons relieved the stark simplicity. MCLAUGHLIN.

A vastly successful dress from the Profile Collection, *opposite*. In grey crêpe, tiny corrugated pleats wrapped and shaped the bodice and fell, column-like, towards the floor. MCLAUGHLIN.

For evening, a long wool crêpe dress went under a deeply Vee-necked jacket, *above*. Understated and stark. MCLAUGHLIN.

The new Profile line for this heavily embroidered, strapless evening dress, *below*, that hugged the body and emphasized the hips. Note the stole; it became a popular Fifties accessory. RANDALL.

Dior's striking new Profile skirt, *right*, jutted over the hips for this immensely popular dress in grey moiré with tightly moulded bodice and long sleeves. With a cheeky pillbox hat and long gloves. MCLAUGHLIN.

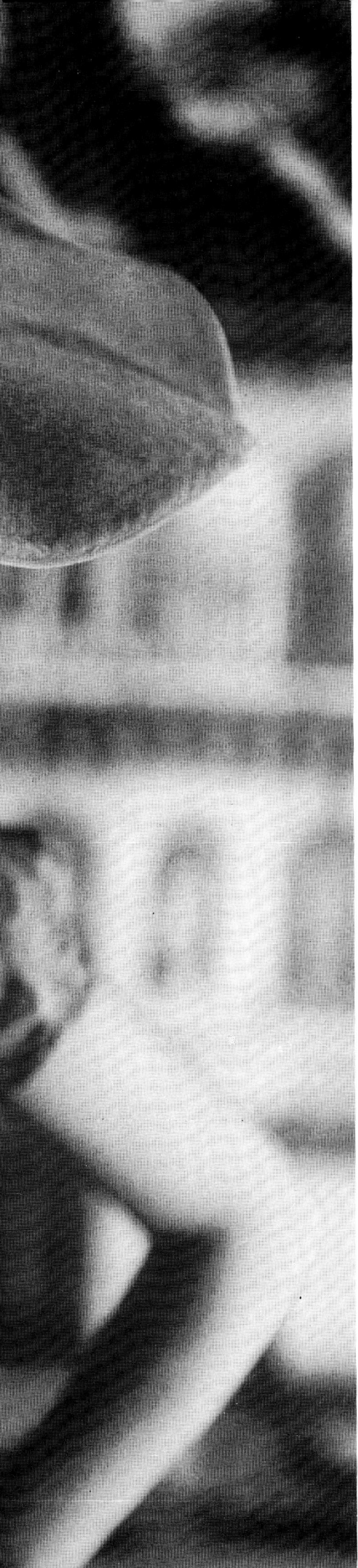

1953

TULIP AND CUPOLA

Given a heady enough mixture of clothes to look at, fashion journalists can almost outdo wine connoisseurs in flowery prose. *Vogue* was intoxicated by the prettiness of the Paris Collections for spring 1953: it compared them to 'a burst of colour .... a real spring with flowers and birds and sea and sun', and, most lyrical of all, 'a delicious promise of lightness, as if every dress were made for the first warm spring day with fat white clouds and a blue sky and a slight breeze to walk against.'

SPRING
With all this talk of nature and flowers, it was appropriate for Dior to launch his Tulip line that season. *Vogue* described it as 'a long stalk of a body, rounding out at the bust and shoulders in petal-shaped curves', and that, more or less, says it all. The Tulip line was a combination of the Profile line of the previous season and Dior's favourite Princesse line. The clothes moulded the body from the hem to just under the bust and from there, by means of padding, puffed sleeves or off-the-shoulder necklines, the width of the bust and shoulders was emphasized. Waists were shaped in but not marked with belts or even seams, and, in fact, Dior commented later that 'little by little waists were being freed'. All in all it was a curvy, feminine, young Collection with no unpleasant surprises: Dior saved these for later.

AUTUMN
At the end of July 1953 he showed his Autumn Collection, unexpectedly triggering off what one newspaper dubbed 'the biggest fashion flapdoodle in years'. He

Dior's Tulip line was padded and curved out round the bust to emphasize the top heavy-look. The flower-printed dress had a wide neck. CLARKE.

101

raised the hemline by two inches to 16 or 17 inches above the ground, or, working the other way, to only a couple of inches below the knee. 'The "Champ" of the Paris dress shows – Christian Dior – floored his rivals today with one surprise knock-out blow. He brought back the short skirt,' said London's *Daily Express*, pointing out that the blow was all the more stunning for being delivered by Dior, the man who had put women into ankle-length skirts six years before. Oh, the fickleness of fashion designers!

A journalist, interviewing Dior the day after the news broke, asked him whether he really thought the new hemline would catch on. Dior is reported to have chortled in reply: 'Didn't you see them yesterday in my salon? They were all trying their skirts at knee-level. They tell me that in the hotels, the visitors are already sending out their skirts and dresses to be shortened.'

The hemline story stayed in the headlines for almost a week, but it appears that, in reality, Dior himself was baffled by all the excitement. 'My astonishment today is as great as that in 1947. I made the dresses that I felt like making, and in the proportions that seemed normal to me.' He criticized the public for paying far too much attention to skirt lengths: 'The length of the skirt does not exist as an element all by itself. The good length begins just where the calf begins to thin down. May each woman look at her legs and find the length that suits her best.' French *Vogue*, which gave an entire page of advice on the new short skirt, agreed. 'NO – it is not shocking or vulgar if each woman adapts it to suit her own age, her type, and above all, her calves.'

The 'flapdoodle' over the hemline rather ousted news about the rest of the show. Dior called his Autumn Collection the *Cupola*, or Dome, line: there were wide, barrel-shaped coats and jackets with exaggeratedly round shoulders, some delicious dresses with full busts and bell skirts, and a new, rounded 'bustle' back for evening dresses, both short and long. But the beltless, high-waisted Princesse dresses held their own too, with waists less marked than ever before.

Dior padded the grey flannel dress, *above*, from shoulder to bosom to give it the new rounded top that he wanted for his Tulip line. The waist curved in but was not marked by a belt or even a seam. CLARKE.

The black alpaca suit, *opposite*, had what *Vogue* called 'the inflated bodice' of Dior's new Tulip line. It was padded and had short puffed sleeves to emphasize the width at the top. The waist was closely moulded and slid into a straight stem skirt. CLARKE.

The dress, *above*, in charcoal grey
flannel had high pockets on the bust
and rounded shoulders to give a top-heavy
Tulip line. The skirt was stem-slim and had
a spotted handkerchief in one pocket and a
crisp white piqué *gilet* at the neck. The waist
was moulded but unbelted. CLARKE.

Dior invented all sorts of wide
necklines to give his Tulip line
evening dresses a top-heavy look. The one in
black, *right*, had its straps going right off the
shoulders and the bodice was cut to make the
bust look high and wide. CLARKE.

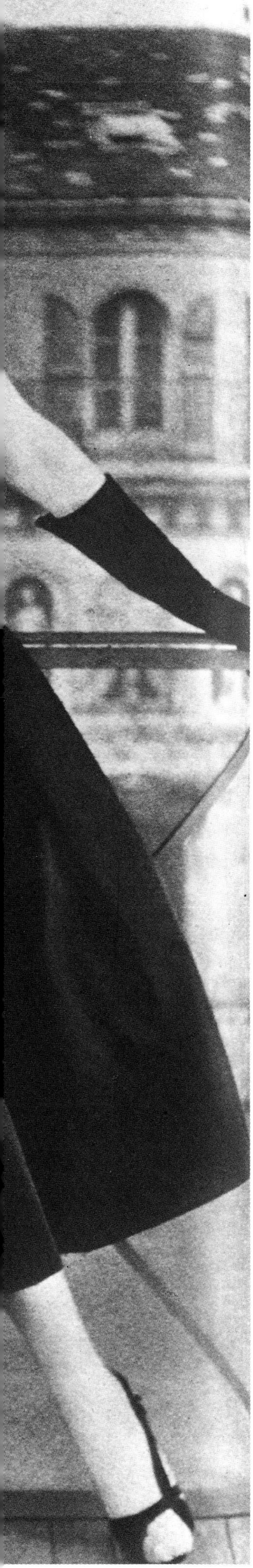

Dior's popular double 'widow's peak' hat, *below*, was in black velvet and grosgrain. CLARKE. Other versions had only one point that dipped down over the forehead. Another popular hat that season was the swathed turban, *right*, in chiffon, tilted down low over the forehead. CLARKE.

A Dior ball dress in satin, *opposite*, with a wide belt giving the feeling of a high waist. Strapless, with an embroidered organdie coat as a cover up. CLARKE.

Vogue said that 'Prints at Dior have always been so pretty that one has to be a raving beauty to be noticed.' They liked this one, *above*, in beige and pink best. The dress had the typical high bust, wide square neck and short sleeves of the Tulip line. CLARKE.

The evening dress in black and white silk organdie, *right*, had the off-the-shoulder neckline and tiny puffed sleeves that Dior used for his Tulip line Collection. The full skirt stopped just above the ankles. CLARKE.

VOGUE

Country weekend wardrobe

Young career clothes

Travel in the sun

Beauty for new fashions

JANUARY 1944   PRICE 3/6

Bouché

Dior's new shorter skirt was a great news story. It appeared in the *Cupola*, or Dome, Collection which gave coats and jackets a wide, rounded barrel shape. Typical were the grey and white tweed, *near right*, and the silk taffeta, *far right*. Both had bows at the front.

The *Cupola* line for autumn 1953 meant big, barrel-shaped coats with inset belts and bows. The red one, *above*, appeared on the cover of *Vogue* later that winter. BOUCHÉ.

Under the *Cupola* jackets and coats went slim sheath dresses with high Princesse bust lines and less defined waistlines than ever before. The one in grey flannel, *right*, was typical. RAWLINGS.

The new skirt that caused the fashion 'flapdoodle', *below. Vogue* chose this one to make their point – it was 16″ from the floor and made of tiers of grey alpaca falling in unpressed pleats. BOUCHÉ.

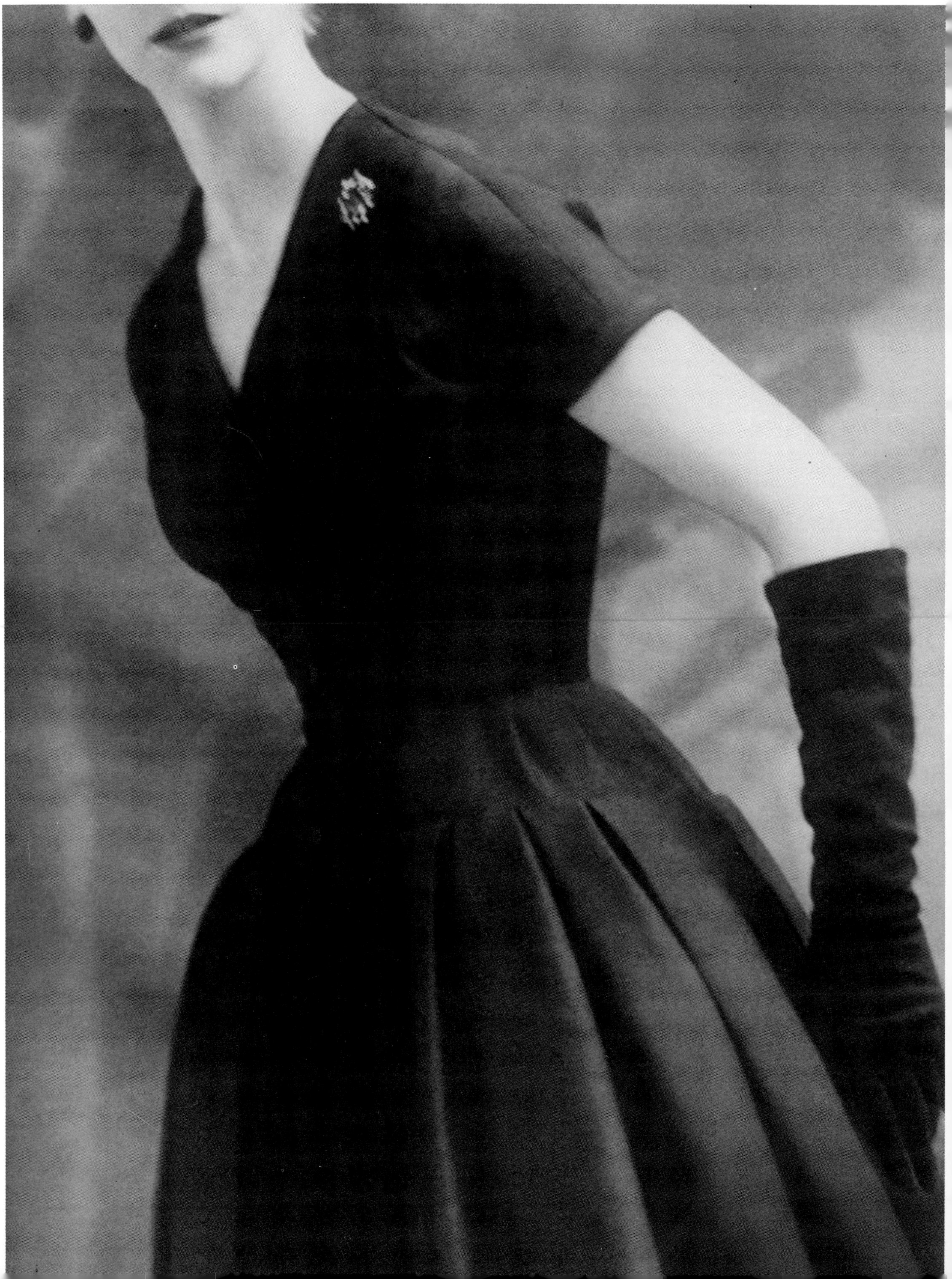

The *Cupola* coat was widely copied; this version, *below*, (by Silhouette de Luxe) was in black and white tweed. DEAKIN. Dior loved jet for the autumn 1953. *Below left*, his favourite jet-beaded pillbox for the evening, worn with jet earrings and choker. CLARKE.

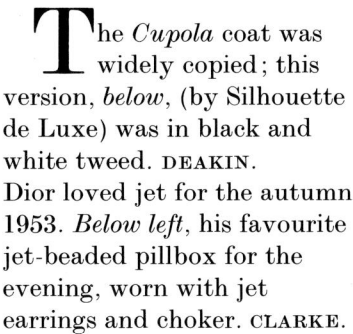

Dior's *Cupola* dresses were marvellously feminine with wide skirts of unpressed pleats and full busts. The dress, *above*, was in grey with a jet necklace and brooch at the waist. RAWLINGS.
The black dress, *opposite*, had a brooch on the shoulder. Both were in wool, a new idea for late day dresses. RANDALL.

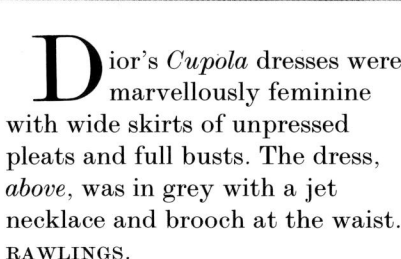

For the evening the *Cupola* line
meant a new fullness at the
back of dresses – almost like a bustle. The
short version, *below*, was in white satin with
a huge bow on the back and a matching
cape. The rose headdress worn with this
dress became very popular. RAWLINGS.

A very dignified version of the
Cupola line, *right*, in black
and white satin with a draped scarf neckline
and a contrasting white satin band at thigh
level. RAWLINGS.

1954

LILY OF THE VALLEY AND H LINE

The talk of Paris in early 1954 was the comeback of the legendary designer Coco Chanel. Mademoiselle Chanel had been enormously successful before the War, but she had closed her doors in 1939 and now she was an old lady of 71. No one could visualize her Thirties clothes in the context of the Fifties, and the fashion world was bursting with curiosity to see what she would come up with. Chanel herself made it seem that her return to the couture was really something she was doing out of a sense of duty – to save her sisters from the excesses of the male couturiers, who were torturing the human body into all sorts of ridiculous shapes simply to promote their own egos. 'Fifties horrors' is how she described the clothes of her rivals.

Chanel had one fashion philosophy: that clothes should be dateless, ageless, relaxed, unexaggerated and, above all, easy to wear. The Collection she showed in 1954 was all of those things, and indeed was hardly different from the one she had shown 15 years before. She did not even try to fit in with the Fifties. The audiences were stunned, and *Vogue* reported that opinion in Paris was violently divided on the Chanel question. *Vogue* itself played safe by praising her 'easy liveable look', while criticizing her for repeating the lines she had made famous in the Thirties without translating them into contemporary terms.

Meanwhile, the extraordinary telepathy that often exists between designers – which makes them think along the same lines without ever, of course, exchanging ideas – was at work in Paris. Or perhaps the couturiers themselves were more aware of the impact Chanel

In the Collections for spring 1954 white was the favourite evening colour. Dior's white silk dress and matching coat were even accessorized with white beads and earrings. COFFIN.

would have than her audiences. Whatever it was, for spring that year the designers produced the most relaxed and casual clothes they had ever made.

SPRING

Dior's Spring Collection was delicious. He called it his Lily of the Valley line after his lucky flower and, like the lily, it was young, pretty, fresh and unsophisticated. There were relaxed little suits with pleated skirts and short, sailor-collared jackets or bloused battledress tops. There were crisp coats with double-breasted fronts and deep vents at the back. There were flowers in button-holes, jaunty straw boaters or sailor hats, and shoes with a new, lower 'Louis' heel. Above all, there was the men's suiting cloth that Dior used again and again – a navy blue, chalk-striped flannel, which somehow looked marvellously feminine tailored into his dapper new day clothes. The waist was less emphasized than ever before: the clothes 'couldn't be easier', said *Vogue* appreciatively.

AUTUMN

Audiences had been charmed by the Lily of the Valley line, but in July, when Dior showed his H line Collection for autumn, controversy raged around the house once again.

Dior's aim with the H line was to suggest 'the tapering figure of a young girl', by stretching the body out a little and elongating the distance between bosom and hips. He pushed the bust up as high as possible and dropped the waist down to the hips (this line made the cross-bar of the H). But people misunderstood, or perhaps, in the case of the Press, they just saw a good what-does-this-man-Dior-think-he-is type of story. They took the new, high bust line to mean <u>no</u> bust, nick-named the new Collection the 'Runner Bean' line, and cried that Dior had abolished the bosom.

He rather wearily denied the charge: 'It had never been my intention to create a flat fashion which would evoke the idea of a runner bean.' *Vogue* leapt to his defence: 'A flattened bust line? You've read about it, perhaps said no to it as un-wise, unflattering. But Dior is not defying nature: rather re-shaping it a little, perhaps beginning a great change...'

Day clothes at Dior followed the new, long-bodied line, but it was the evening wear that carried it to its extreme. The long, tight ballerina bodice that caused most of the fuss was christened the 'Degas' look by *Vogue*, which recommended it to its slimmer readers, while his other controversial bodice shape it named the 'Tudor', because it bandaged the breasts so high and tight that they swelled above the dress in two globes 'like an Anne Boleyn portrait'. This, they advised, would make 'any woman with a fuller figure look younger, more romantic.'

Dior tried to emphasize that the H line was more than an argument about where and how the bust should be: it marked, he said, 'the liberation of the waist', something he had been leading up to in previous Collections. This was certainly a major turning point in fashion and both *Vogue* and its rival, *Harper's Bazaar*, took it very seriously. (*Harper's* fashion editor cabled back to America: 'the H line represents an even more important development than the New Look.') *Vogue* proclaimed: 'A new woman is born ... 1954's woman has straight shoulders, a high bust, trim hips and a slim but unexaggerated waist. She is a woman of her time. Her clothes are sober and supple, liberated from useless detail.' The words could equally have been describing a Chanel Collection but it was Dior's H line they were writing about. '*Vogue* applauds the charm of this new woman and predicts success and happiness for her.'

In November of that year, Dior took his H line Collection to England for a charity gala at Blenheim Palace, with an audience of 1,600 and with Princess Margaret as guest of honour. It was three months since the Collection had been launched in Paris, but the Press reported that 'the first appearance of the H line seemed to stun the audience into silence.' It took 25 minutes of models parading up and down the catwalk before people started applauding, but by the end of the show the audience was captivated.

For this Collection Dior used men's suiting material – navy blue chalk-striped flannel – with enormous success. Here tailored into a neat little battle blouse top, worn over a dress with camisole bodice and pleated skirt. CLARKE.

The jaunty new look from Dior, *above*. This dress, in his popular navy striped flannel, had a gently bloused top and a white linen collar that knotted like a sailor's in the front. CLARKE.

For the spring of 1954 Dior's new coat, *opposite*, was as dapper as the grey chalk-striped flannel it was made in. Double-breasted with long revers and a deep vent at the back, it was worn with a pert boater and crisp white gloves. Heels were lower. CLARKE.

The softly bloused dress in grey alpaca, *right*, was teamed with accessories in Dior's perennial favourite, navy blue. CLARKE.

The navy blue dress, *above*, had the short youthful bloused jacket that appeared in spring 1954. This one in navy satin was teamed with a sailor hat. CLARKE.

Dior's new sailor look, *left*. In navy wool, the jacket had a sailor tie in the front. The brooch pinned at the top of the arm gave it a real Navy flash. CLARKE.

By coincidence, in the year of Chanel's comeback to couture, one of Dior's popular suits in navy jersey, *above*, had a Chanel look. CLARKE.

Boaters and sailor hats were favourites at Dior that spring. *Top*, a traditional shape trimmed with a velvet ribbon. CLARKE. *Above*, a boater brim with a soft crown in black silk. *Vogue* called it his 'Henry VIII' hat. CLARKE.

One of Dior's prettiest ideas, *right*, a fine white handkerchief lawn jacket, pleated and softly bloused over a grey silk dress. Dior filled in the neckline with strings of white beads. The idea caught on fast. CLARKE.

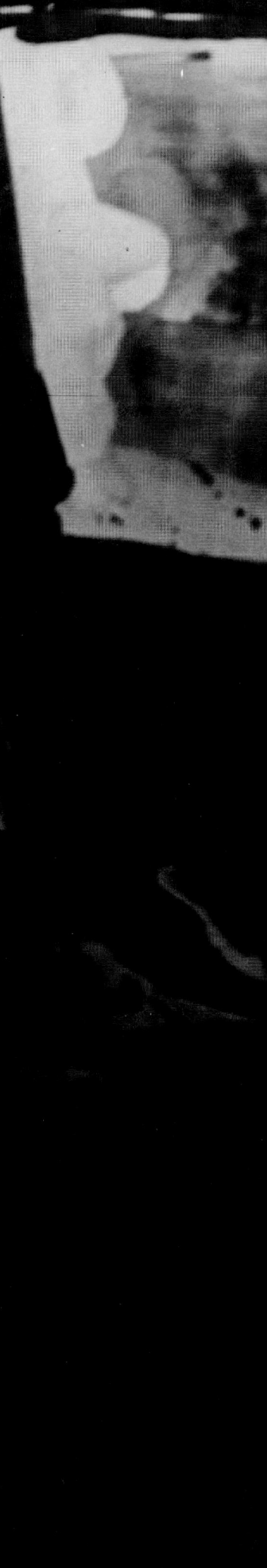

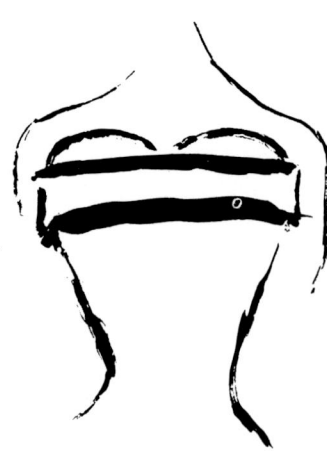

From the controversial H line Collection, Dior's daring 'Tudor' bodice as represented by *Vogue*, *right*. The Tudor bodice pushed the bust up so high that it swelled above the dress 'like an Anne Boleyn portrait', said *Vogue*. ERIC. The Tudor bodice appeared on the apricot silk evening dress, *left*. COFFIN.

The new high bust and long body that Dior introduced for his H line was particularly pronounced on evening clothes. *Vogue's* representation of the 'Degas' bodice, *below*, was like the top of a ballerina's costume – long, tight, pushing the bust up high and flat. It moulded the waist without exaggeration and the skirt started on the hips. ERIC.

Opposite, the 'young girl' figure that Dior wanted to achieve with his H line. Pretty in pearl grey satin with pearls in the hair and on the bow. The big skirt started from the new waistline. COFFIN. The same Degas bodice was on the grey/beige satin evening dress, *right*. The wide skirt came from the hip. COFFIN.

The new H line in grey/green tweed, *left*. The jacket was long, double-breasted and only slightly curved in at the waist. It had narrow, straight shoulders and a slender skirt. A sprig of Dior's lucky flower, lily of the valley, was tucked into the buttonhole. COFFIN.

Another example of the long H line jacket, this time in black and rust herringbone, *above*. The suit was worn with the collar up and a big-brimmed feather hat. COFFIN.
The double-breasted H line coat, *above left*, with the new high bustline, gentle curve into the waist and slim bell skirt. COFFIN.

The H line for day, autumn 1954. The three-piece in black and white tweed, *right*, had a new long jacket that was only just shaped in to indicate a waist. It went over a straight skirt and an easy top that sat neatly on the hips. COFFIN. According to *Vogue*, everyone who saw this long-bodied new suit in brown wool, *above*, wanted one. CLARKE.

The Degas bodice of the H line, *above*, on a pale blue tulle evening dress embroidered with silver. COFFIN.

With its long bodice and slender skirt, the elegant black silk dress, *above right*, illustrated the H line perfectly. The dropped waist and the gently gathered peplum marked the cross-bar of the letter H. COFFIN.

A daring red chiffon dress, *opposite left*, with the new Tudor bodice. It was worn with a coat of taffeta and had a belt to match. COFFIN.

Dior's H line for an evening dress in pale pink satin, *above right*. In this case the dropped waist was marked by a huge bow. COFFIN.
The new shoe from Dior – lower with a waisted 'Louis' heel. WEISS.

1955

A LINE AND Y LINE

The initial hostility to the H line of the previous season evaporated when women saw how pretty it really was, and by the time Dior showed his next Collection in spring 1955, the H line had become an accepted fashion.

SPRING

That spring, Dior developed the H line into the A line – a look that was to be even more successful and influential. He narrowed the shoulders and made dresses, coats and suits flare out like triangles, with the waists – the cross-bar of the letter A – up under the bust or low on the hips. Dior's A line represented everything he was best at: a strong theme – but one that made women look feminine and pretty – and one that could be copied fairly easily and still look right. Everyone loved it: 'The most wanted silhouette in Paris,' *Vogue* called it, adding wittily, 'the prettiest triangle since Pythagoras.'

The A line and its predecessor, the H line, were revolutionary. They marked a complete U-turn in fashion, away from the nipped-in waists and full skirts of the New Look to a sleeker, almost waistless shape that, in turn, opened the door to the sack and the shift, which have been with us in one guise or another ever since. ('A line' went straight into the fashion vocabulary: 26 years later you can still describe a triangular skirt or dress as being A line and people know exactly what you mean.)

This was a high point, a heyday, for the Paris

The straps of this Dior black silk evening dress made a discreet Y for his Autumn Y line Collection. The hem of the dress rose in front and dipped into a train at the back. CLARKE.

designers. No reputable journalist or buyer could afford to miss the Collections, for their influence on fashion was unchallenged. According to *Vogue*, the designers had by now split into two rival camps: there were those – led by Dior – who believed in producing clothes of so strong a shape and character that they looked as if they could 'walk across the room alone'. The other camp, which had Balenciaga and Chanel as its king and queen, simply believed in designing elegant clothes with the sole purpose of making women look more beautiful.

The ready-to-wear manufacturers had no doubts as to which camp to follow – that led by Dior, producing clothes of 'character'. These clothes had a look which could be easily defined and copied. You knew where you were with Dior's dresses; you knew what was in fashion and what was out. The clothes of Balenciaga and Chanel were more difficult to translate successfully into ready-to-wear fashion; so much depended on exquisite cut and the sort of subtle touches that are desperately expensive to reproduce. Chanel's cardigan suit was, of course, hugely influential, but it only really looked its best when made from superb tweed, quilted onto its silk lining and given other Chanel touches – for example, the chain in the hem to make it hang correctly. And in any case, Chanel might produce only one suit, whereas Dior created something different every season.

Purists have always considered Balenciaga and Chanel the creative geniuses of Paris, the intellectuals of fashion, but there was no one to compete with Dior when it came to capturing the imagination of the Press and public. One has only to mention Dior to people who lived through the Fifties and they will smile and nostalgically reminisce about the A line, the H line and the New Look; but talk about Balenciaga and only among the true fashion *cognoscenti* will there be any response at all.

AUTUMN

For his Autumn Collection that year, Dior went to the alphabet again, skipping from the first letter, A, to the second last, Y. The Y line was less easy to pinpoint than the A, but basically it was defined as a slender body with a top-heavy look. This Dior achieved by adding big collars that

opened up in a V shape, like the arms of the Y, with giant stoles swathed about the shoulders or with cropped bolero jackets topping ultra-slim dresses. The Y could be upside down too: long tunics with deep slits up the sides. These were so waistless and easy that they were really early sacks or shifts (as this shape came to be called later).

Another important group of clothes were the ones inspired by oriental costumes. Dior showed puffed harem skirts, dresses like Chinese *cheongsams*, and long, side-slit caftans. Within ten years fashion was to go on an ethnic binge – it's nice to speculate that perhaps Dior saw it coming.

The suit that told the whole story of Dior's A line Collection for spring 1955, *right*. The tunic jacket was narrow across the shoulders but flared out towards the hem, giving the illusion of an A shape. GRUAU.

The A line for evening, *far right*. A black silk *faille* tunic and skirt. The square-necked tunic skimmed the waist to sweep over the stiffened, wide skirt. Underneath the tunic was a dress of the same shape with tiny, shoestring straps. GORMAN.

A soft suit in grey flannel, *opposite*, with the easiest jacket and a pleated skirt. This was the A line at its least exaggerated and most appealing. The new cross-bar shoes became extremely popular too. RADKAI.

D ior did not abandon the H line altogether, but exaggerated it by making the jackets less fitted than ever – as in the suit, *right*. RADKAI.

A typical version of the A line, *below*, with neat narrow shoulders on a grey flannel tunic jacket that flared out in a triangular shape over the pleated skirt. CLARKE.

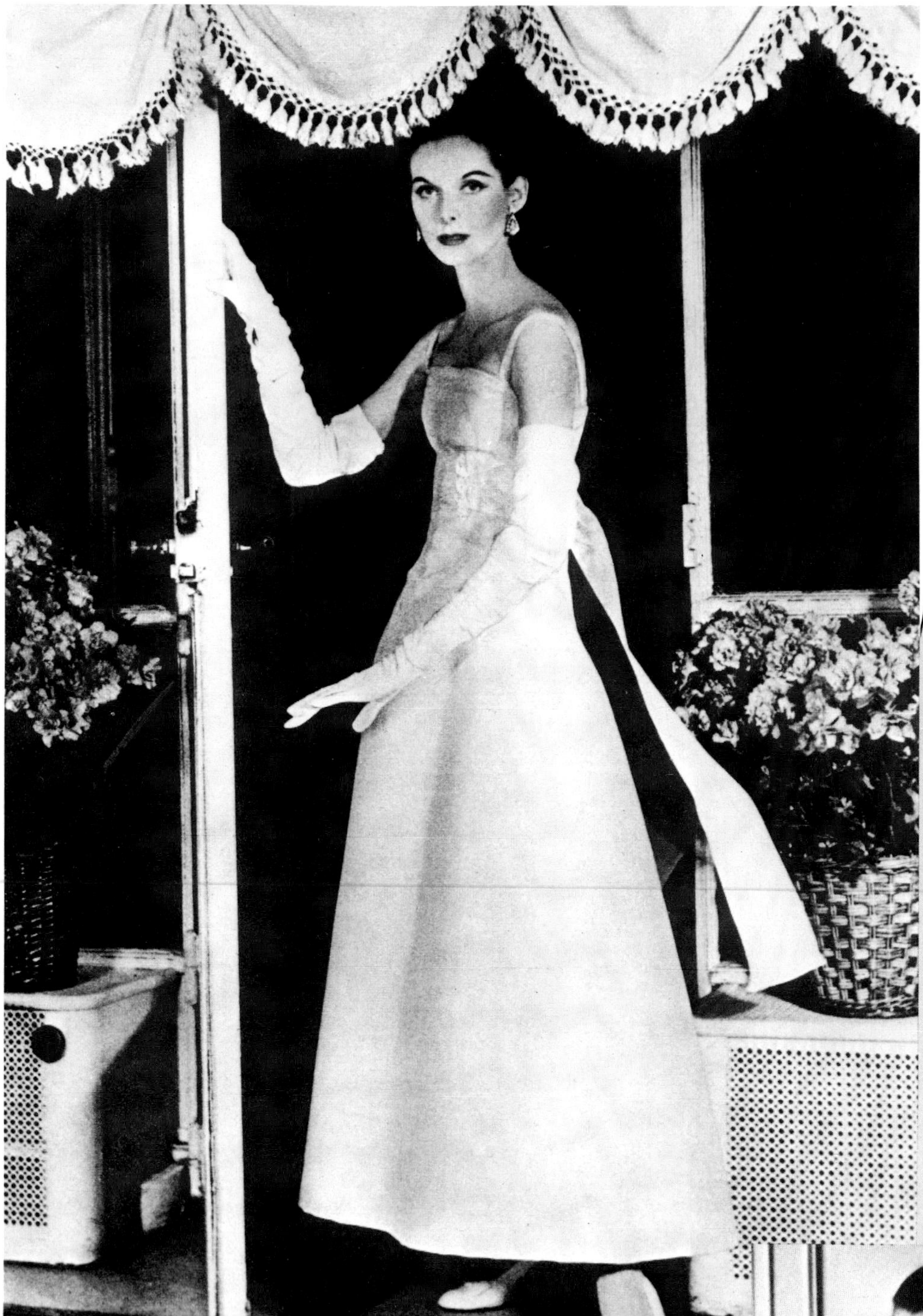

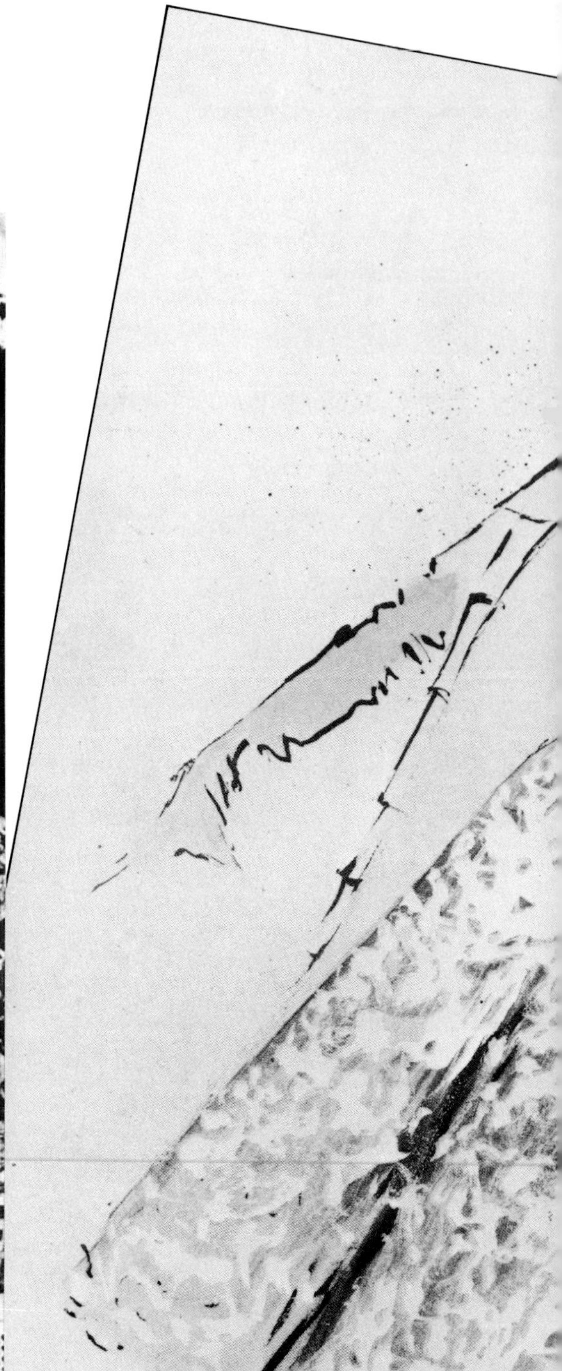

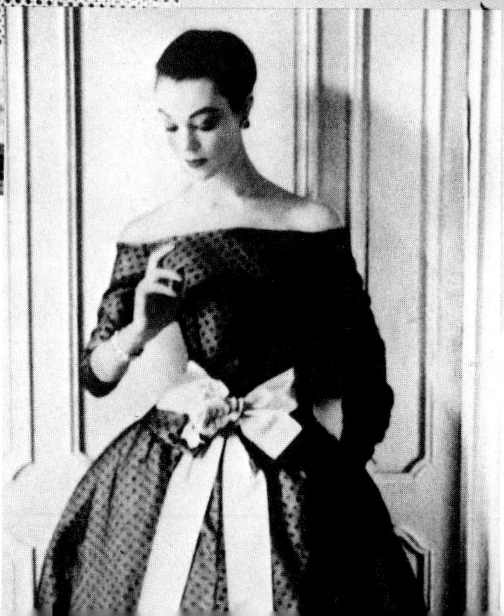

The bodice on the white organza evening dress, *far left*, was high and flat with a sash caught up by a fall of rhinestones. The triangular skirt was mounted on white satin. RADKAI.

A grand ball dress in black silk, *below left*, with an enormous bow in blue satin. The dropped waistline was typical of the A and Y lines. CLARKE.

The A line evening dress, *centre*, was in white lace with a sash under the bust. The tiered coat was in white organdie.

From Dior's A line Collection: a ravishing young girl's dress, *above*, in white organdie with his favourite lilies of the valley at the high waist. CLARKE.

Dior's Y line meant a slender body with a top-heavy look. He achieved this in various ways; one was to wrap a bulky stole round the shoulders. This one, *right*, buttoned onto the back of the high-necked slim dress it went with. *Vogue* said it was hard to tell if Dior's new stoles should be called collars or stoles. They decided that it was a collar if it buttoned at the front. CLARKE. The stole, *above*, did not just button, it was double-breasted. CLARKE.

Another way of achieving a Y line was to put on a collar whose revers became the arms of the letter Y. That is what Dior did with the simple, fly-fronted dress, *left*, in black and white herringbone tweed. He also padded out the shoulders to get width at the top. CLARKE.

Another trick was to put a short, chunky bolero jacket over a narrow dress. The one, *above*, in black and white tweed was extra bulky as it was lined in beaver. CLARKE.

139

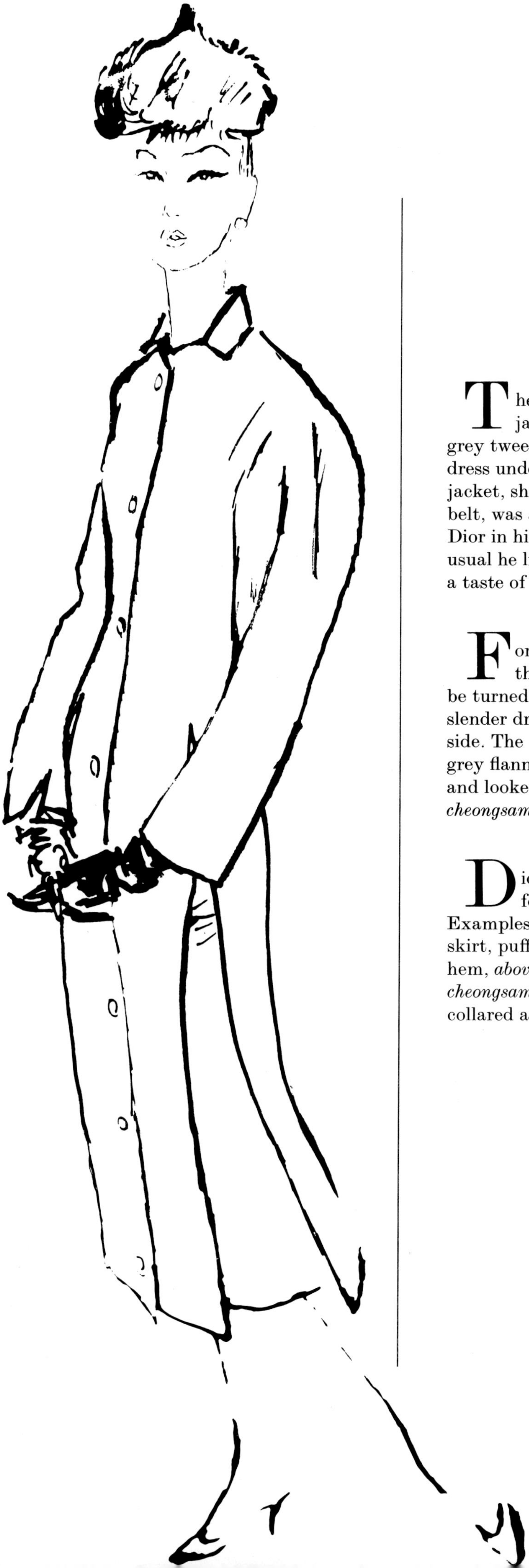

The cropped-off bolero jacket, *opposite*, was in grey tweed with a full-skirted dress underneath. This kind of jacket, short enough to reveal the belt, was a favourite theme for Dior in his next Collection, and as usual he liked to give his audience a taste of the future. BOUCHÉ.

For another kind of look, the Y of Dior's line could be turned upside down: a long slender dress or caftan slit up the side. The daytime version, *left*, in grey flannel had slits to the waist and looked like a Chinese *cheongsam*. BOUCHÉ.

Dior liked the oriental look for the autumn 1955. Examples included the new harem skirt, puffed out above a hobble hem, *above right*, and the Chinese *cheongsam* dress, *below right*, high-collared and slim. BOURET.

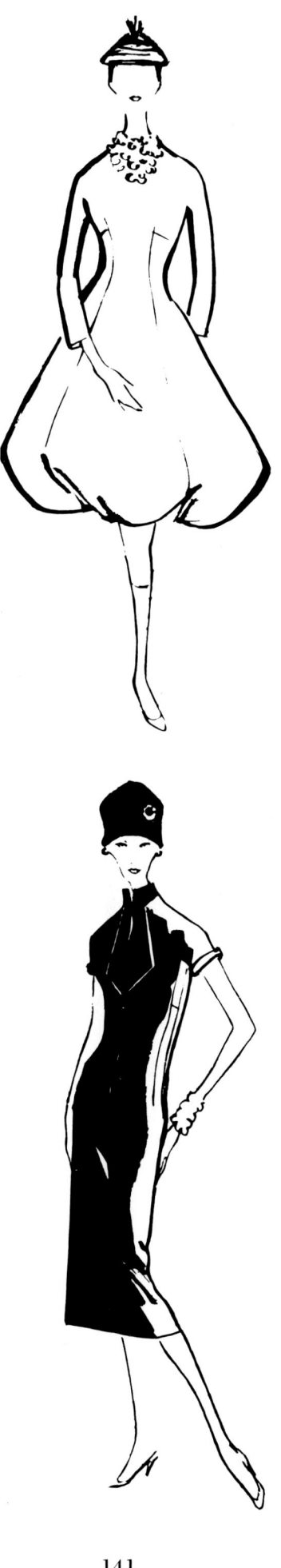

Dior's loose overblouse, *above*, slit deeply so that the dress below could be seen, served the same purpose as his bolero jackets – it added width to the top. This version was in satin with a diamanté brooch. CLARKE.

Exotic oriental splendour in the lushly printed satin coat, *below right*, lined in mink, over a matching dress and worn with a silk turban. CLARKE.

Dior's Japanese *obi* sash tied tightly under the high bosom of the pearl grey satin evening dress, *above right*. One end of the sash went over the shoulder to form a sort of half stole. CLARKE.

Another rich and rare evening coat, *far right*, in red velvet worn with a jewelled necklace, earrings and a turban hat. CLARKE.

1956

ARROW AND AIMANT

In 1956 Dior published his autobiography. The original French edition was, curiously, called *Christian Dior and me by Christian Dior*, but in the prologue of the book Dior explained that it was not really so much *his* story as that of another fellow altogether – Christian Dior the couturier, a nine-year-old phenomenon who had come to dominate his life.

Dior was bothered by the dual personality that success had inflicted upon him. Ever since the unexpected triumph of his first Collection, he had found it difficult to reconcile the naturally shy and private side of his nature – his 'shrinking' side – with the showman and extrovert his business demanded of him. Dior, the private man, loved nothing better than caring for the garden in his lovely old mill house near the Forest of Fontainebleau. 'I like all the simple things of life, such as small parties of old friends; I detest the noise and bustle of the world and sudden, violent changes.' But Christian Dior, the couturier, was very different: 'Ensconced in a magnificent house in the Avenue Montaigne, he is a compound of people, dresses, stockings, perfumes, publicity handouts, press photographs and, every now and then, a small bloodless (but inky!) revolution whose reverberations are felt all over the world.'

SPRING
Back in the 'magnificent house on the Avenue Montaigne', a new Collection was shown for spring

F rom Dior's Arrow Collection: a supple top, tightly fitting the silhouette with a self-belt. Made of gabardine, the suit was typically worn with a sprig of lily of the valley. CLARKE.

1956. *Vogue* loved it: 'Not since 1947 and Dior's famous first Collection have Paris fashions had such a rush of femininity – nor have there been so many *bravos* at the dramatic end of an opening.'

Like so many of Dior's Spring Collections, this one radiated gentle prettiness rather than revolution. (Perhaps spring touched the soul of the private, country-loving Dior rather than the showman.) He called the Collection the Arrow line, and showed two new versions of the high waist that he had loved since his Princesse line. This time, there were what he called 'Caraco' jackets, chopped off above the waist to show the belt of the dress underneath, and young and jaunty in spirit. The other, more womanly, look had loose-cut jackets caught in with a belt or sash well above the waist and worn over slim skirts.

He still liked the straight, side-slit tunic dresses that he had shown the previous autumn, but only for evening. It was almost as if he was marking time with this revolutionary idea until the moment was ripe to launch it properly: that moment came in time for his last Collection.

Like all the Paris designers that season, Dior liked adding crisp touches of white to his outfits: white piqué waistcoats, frothy white organdie or chiffon blouses under suits, white collars. Altogether it was agreed that it was an extraordinarily pretty collection.

AUTUMN

The private man gave way to the showman in the Autumn Collection. The man who had lengthened hems to the ankle in 1947, and then shortened them to below the knee in 1953, now abruptly produced daytime suits with skirts as long as those of an Edwardian lady. To be fair, there were only six of them in a Collection that took two hours to show, but it was enough to set tongues wagging and typewriters clacking. 'Dior's explosive *demi-longueur*,' *Vogue* exclaimed, 'hailed, laughed at, sighed after, feared, endlessly discussed. Is it a stunt or a serious development? Should we, can we, do we, want to revert to pre-emancipation femininity in the uncompromisingly emancipated era we live in?'

The new line was called *Aimant*, or Loving, and the clothes were romantic in feeling and full of nostalgia for a past age. 'The look that harks back to the epoch of Poiret and Proust,' *Vogue* called it. Apart from the long hems, Dior swaddled his mannequins in capes of all lengths, cocooned them in cape coats, wrapped them in fur, shadowed their pretty faces with hat veils and put them into the most fragile and delicate evening dresses imaginable.

Vogue explained that if fashion were to accept the Edwardian look of capes and fur stoles and widely-rounded shoulders, then it must also see that 'the silhouette cries out for the balance of a lengthened, narrow skirt.' It advised each reader to consider the logic behind the long hems and 'get your eye in. For it may very well be the shape of things to come next year.'

Dior's unfitted jacket caught in above the waist with a belt or tie, and worn with a slim skirt, was a more womanly alternative to the Caraco brief overblouse (see overleaf). This version, *opposite*, was in navy blue silk alpaca. CLARKE.
The Caraco line for evening, *below*. The bodice was cropped above the waist to expose the neat belt. In spotted silk, with a billowing skirt and balloon sleeves. CLARKE.

A young-looking flared jacket, *far left*, from the Spring 1956 Collection. The jacket was cropped just below the waist, and had deep side slits for added movement. CLARKE.

The high-waisted jacket in navy blue wool, *above left*, had a long-ended bow and a deep Vee neck. CLARKE.

Dior's new way with a high waist: the Caraco jacket. It dominated the Spring Collection for 1956. Like a brief overblouse, it was cropped off above the waist to reveal the belt of the dress below. The one, *below left*, was in navy blue wool and had a wrap-over skirt underneath and Dior's new 'Hairdryer' hat on top. CLARKE.

The new high waist for an easy suit in grey Prince of Wales check (a favourite new Paris fabric), *right*. Dior loved to add a dash of white to an outfit. On this suit, the white organdie blouse collar was worn outside the jacket. Another pretty touch – the posy of cornflowers on the lapel. CLARKE.

A favourite Dior touch for the
spring 1956 was a frosting of
white on an outfit – *Vogue* called them
'lingerie touches', as Dior often made
them of organdie or chiffon. The dress,
above, in black silk, had a built-in *fichu*
in white organdie. CLARKE.

A billowing skirt offset the prim,
high neck and long sleeves of
the Dior two-piece dress, *right*, in
brilliant coral colours. It was worn with
a huge picture hat – still a Dior
favourite. CLARKE.

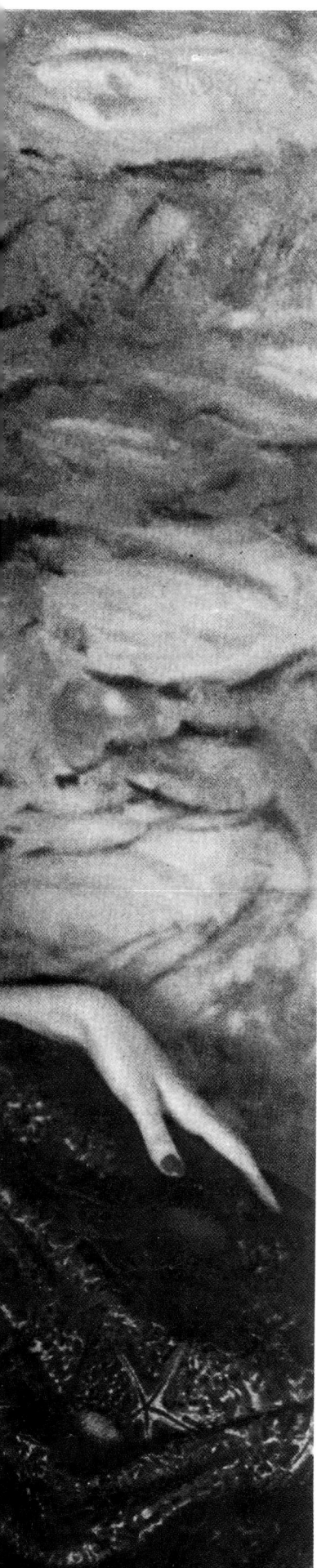

The high waist dominated the
evening look for the spring 1956.
The bare black dress, *above*, had a high
bow and jewelled pendant and was
worn with an enormous black picture
hat. CLARKE.

Dior's stunning dress, *far right*, in flame-coloured chiffon, had the 1956 hallmark of a high waist. CLARKE.

By May 1956 Dior copies had come into the shops in Britain. The example, *right*, was in high-waisted chiffon and sold at $23\frac{1}{2}$ guineas. SILVERSTEIN.

The slender sheath dress, *left*, had a white piqué trim at the neck and a buttoned fold to mark the high waist. CLARKE.

Other examples of Dior copies which appeared in the shops in Britain: *right*, a ready-to-wear Caraco jacket at 18 guineas, and the slender, high-waisted sheath dress, *far left*, at 11 guineas. SILVERSTEIN.

155

The romantic-looking suit, *right*, in red tweed 'for cocktail to dinner evenings', said *Vogue*. The skirt was softly gathered, the jacket short and close-fitting and the collar of the red chiffon blouse underneath made the collar of the outfit. Worn with a red picture hat trimmed with a rose. BOUCHÉ.

For the autumn 1956 Dior showed the new *demi-longueur*, which aroused a great deal of emotion. According to *Vogue* it was in turn, 'hailed, laughed at, sighed after, feared and endlessly discussed'. There were in fact only six of the new length suits shown. Here are two of them. *Opposite left*, in grey and black tweed with a short jacket worn over a black silk jersey blouse and a skirt of unpressed pleats. MCLAUGHLIN. *Opposite right*, in grey tweed with a belted jacket and jabot of white chiffon. MCLAUGHLIN.

The nostalgic Edwardian look, which Dior liked in autumn 1956, included long and short capes. The version, *opposite*, in navy blue wool, fastened with two large buttons and was worn over a matching dress. Note the new high hat. MCLAUGHLIN.

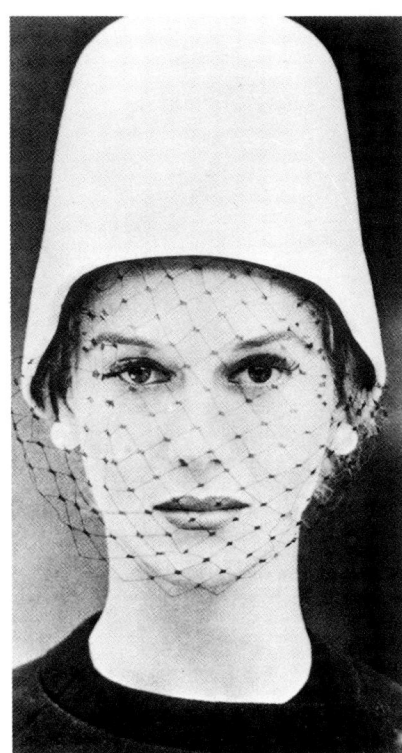

For the winter of 1956, Dior's hats were often veiled, *above*, but they were high, plain and not easy to wear. MCLAUGHLIN.

Dior's new cape-coat. *right*, was double-breasted and wide-cut with stubby sleeves that started at the elbow. In green tweed and worn with a veiled 'pot' hat. MCLAUGHLIN.

Dior's low neckline and high waist came together on this ball dress, *opposite*, in gold lamé organza. MCLAUGHLIN.

Dior's draped chiffon dresses were exquisitely made, marvellously feminine and fragile. The dress, *above*, stressed the high-waisted look. MCLAUGHLIN.

The Edwardian 'My Fair Lady' look that Dior showed for the winter of 1956, *above*. Once again the high waist and the low neck met in the middle. MCLAUGHLIN.

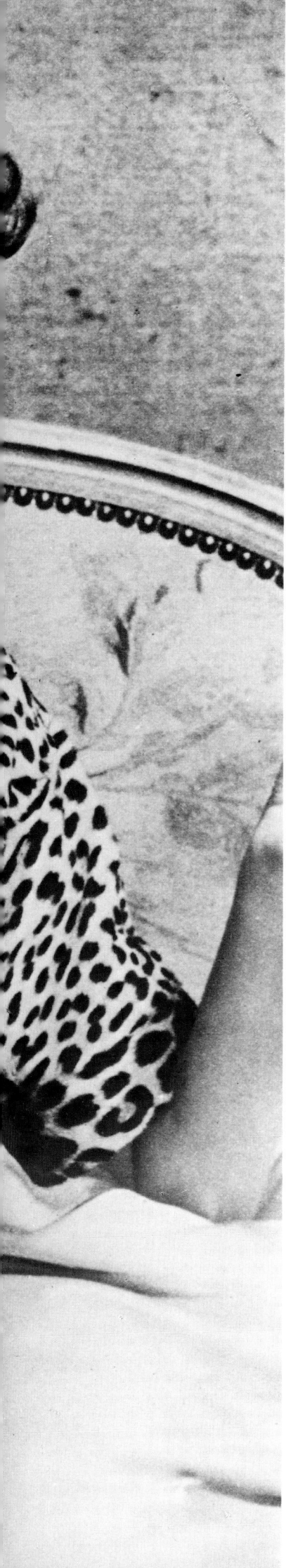

1957

LIBRE AND FUSEAU

With the Collection for spring 1957, the House of Christian Dior celebrated its tenth anniversary. *Vogue* fêted the birthday with a special full-page portrait of Monsieur Dior, paying tribute to those ten years 'during which he has gone on topping himself, showing each season clothes that manage to be simultaneously fresh, witty and full of elegant surprises.'

It looked back (of course) to the dramatic days of the New Look, shown exactly one decade before, which had, it said, more than new cars or nylons or automatic washing machines, given post-war woman 'the real Elysian lift – the smirky, cat-in-cream thing that happens to women in front of mirrors.' It reminisced about the storm that Dior had unwittingly whipped up with his ankle-length, New Look skirts, remembering how some stouthearted women in Texas had formed the Little-Below-the-Knee Club to protect the hem length *they* considered right and proper from the wily Frenchman.

Most importantly, *Vogue* recognized that it was Dior's success with the New Look Collection that had put the French couture back in business after the War. This success had made it impossible for manufacturers in other countries to go it alone; it had forced them to look towards Paris for their direction and inspiration. In that freezing February of 1947 there had only been 18 American buyers at Dior's opening show, but by 1957 the editor of American *Vogue* reported from Paris that 'almost everyone of importance in the fashion world was either present, or represented, at the Collections. All had come to the world's fashion laboratory for information, ideas, and refreshment. Here, in this

Dior's luxury version of the *vareuse* – the fisherman's smock that Breton seamen wear. He cut this one in Somali leopard. CLARKE.

Collections week (on whose success depend the earnings of thousands of French workers), was the living proof that France has something so powerful, so desirable, that the world will travel as far as it must to get it.'

SPRING

Dior's Collection that spring was called *Libre*, or Free, and so it was. Ten years had brought him to the exact opposite of the New Look, with its waist-cinching, padded, structured and elaborately feminine clothes. In fact, Dior based much of his *Libre* line on two classic items of clothing normally worn by *men*. One was the *vareuse*, or fisherman's smock, worn by Breton seamen and which traditionally has a stand-away collar and is cut to hang loosely down to the hips; the other was the khaki bush jacket with its buttoned-down flap pockets. He called his versions of the bush shirt *les Sahariennes* and made them super-elegant in rich raw silk or natural shantung. The *vareuse* he translated in all sorts of ways – most spectacularly he cut it in leopard skin and put it over a tweed skirt.

Dior's favourite colours that season were white, off-white, beige and natural. His model girls wore hats like topees; they had lost the rather doll-like appearance that the New Look had given them: now they all looked like cool colonial ladies or Hemingway heroines. Skirt lengths for day dropped a couple of inches, and the *demi-longueur* that had caused all the fuss the year before was now the popular length for cocktail and dinner dresses. (I remember a tussle with my mother that summer. She wanted to shorten a party dress she had bought me and I was as determined as only a 17-year-old can be to wear it the fashionable 'ballerina' length, as we called it. I had been taken in a school party to the Dior show the previous winter, and considered myself a fashion expert.)

AUTUMN

Dior's last Collection was for autumn 1957. He called it the *Fuseau*, or Spindle, line. No one knew, of course, that this was to be the great designer's finale; Dior's death from a heart attack in October that year was shockingly sudden. But Fate was kind, and allowed him to go out on a Collection as

revolutionary as the one he had come in with.

That autumn, he finally put his seal of approval on the loose chemise shape which had fascinated him for several seasons. This unfitted dress came to be known by many names – the chemise, the chemmy, the tube, the sack, the shift. Like so many of Dior's new ideas, it attracted vociferous critics. They described it as baggy and inelegant, but by September that year French *Vogue* reported that Dior's battle for the loose line had been won: the proof was that women were wearing it. Although *Vogue* insisted it was a difficult fashion and one that should only be attempted by the tall and slender, it was proved wrong: the chemise and its successors became the refuge of all overweight women.

The chemise changed our shapes, it altered the whole direction of fashion, and it paved the way for designers like Courrèges and Mary Quant and the young, free fashions of the Sixties.

As the journalists crowded out of the Dior salon that July morning with yet another good story, and the buyers went home with fodder for six months' fashion, they did not realize that they had witnessed the end of an era – the last ideas of the man who had dominated fashion since the War. There were, of course, to be more fashion stories – indeed, lots of them – about the turbulent changes that would take place at the House of Christian Dior. Nevertheless, the death of Dior was a nail in the coffin of the French couture. The world was changing rapidly and fashion had to reflect those changes. Instead, the fashion world found itself in disarray and confusion, for it had lost its leader.

A slender sheath that skimmed the contours of the body. Dior's new chemise-like dress in lavishly embroidered tulle. From the Spring Collection 1957. CLARKE.

Though the real *vareuse* is a loose garment, Dior liked to belt his versions of it. This one, *left*, was in navy blue wool and the new wide neckline revealed the pale chiffon blouse beneath. CLARKE.

Another example of his *vareuse* top, *right*, looked cool and colonial with its deep topee-shaped hat. CLARKE.

Dior's *Saharienne* suit, *above*, was inspired by the traditional bush jacket. He adapted it in various ways and this one was in natural shantung and had buttons where the four bush jacket pockets would normally go. CLARKE.

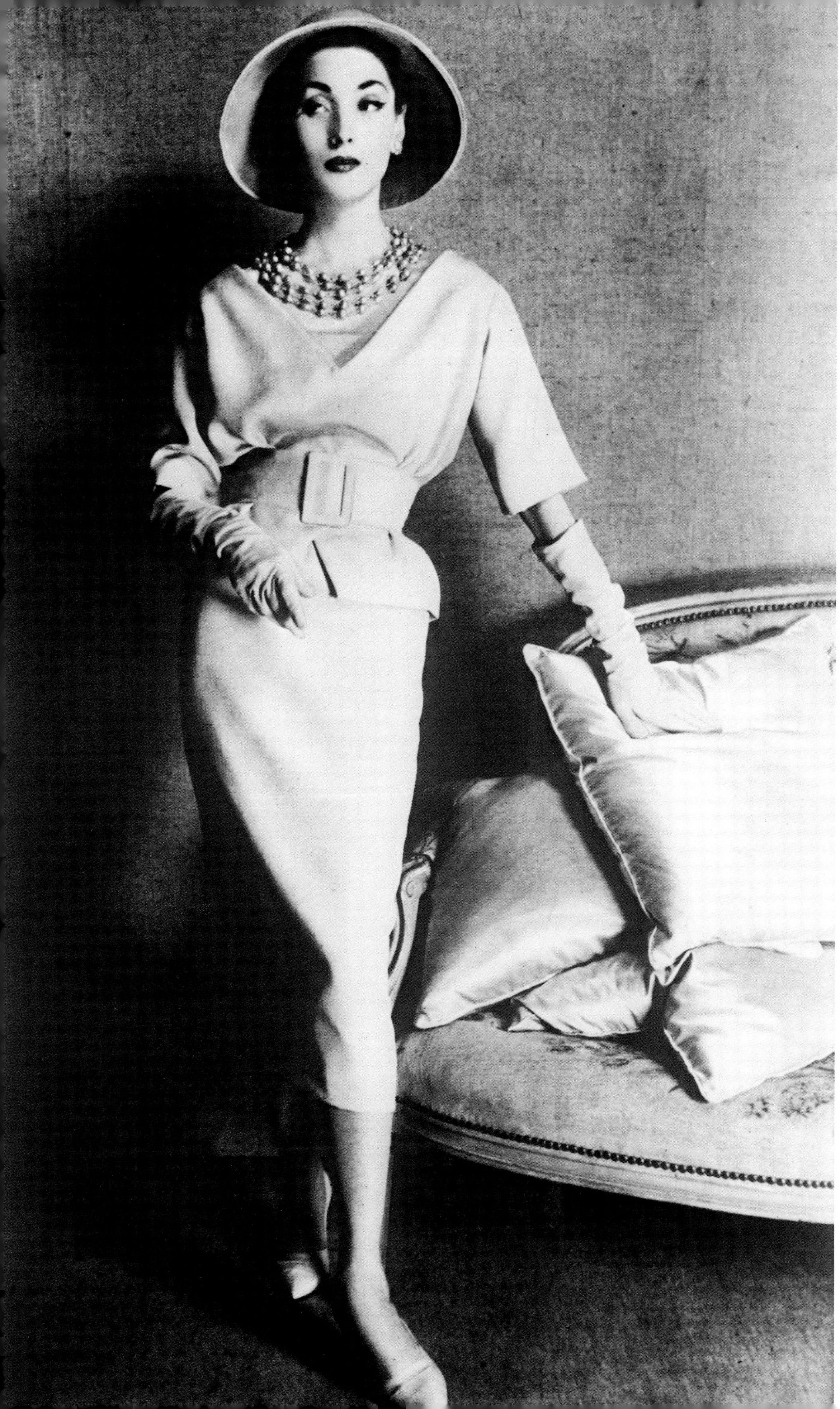

Only a mauve rose tucked into the bodice interrupted the pure white of the silk two-piece dress, *right*, with matching straight coat and soft *fichu* collar. CLARKE.

For the spring of 1957 Dior continued to show the loose oriental-type tunics. This one, *centre*, was in copper brown silk with a tiny geometric print and was worn over a matching straight skirt. The sphinx hat was in black. CLARKE.

Heavy white shantung made the long tunic dress, *far right*, with deep side slits. *Vogue* described it as 'alluring as an ivory tower'. CLARKE.

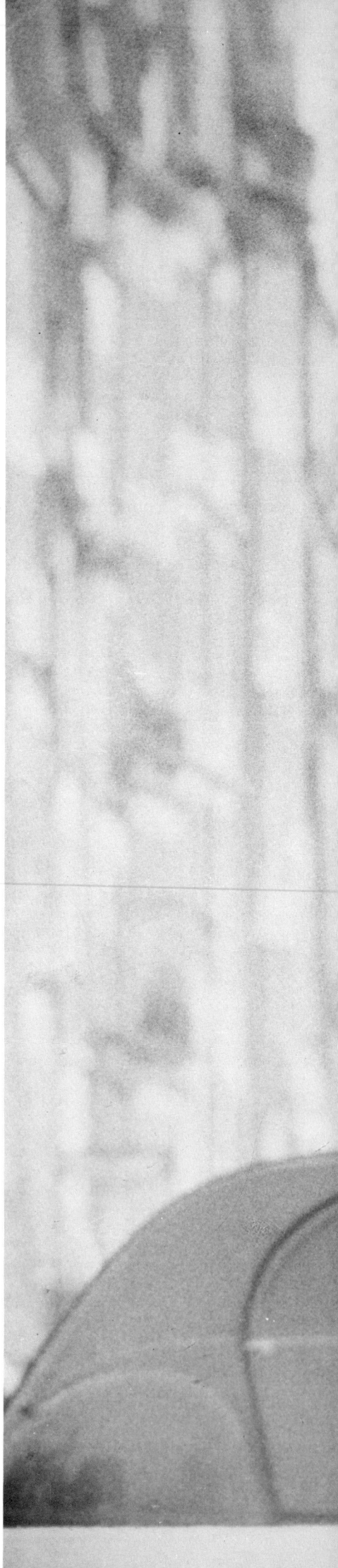

In autumn 1957 – a decade after he launched the controversial New Look – Dior brought out the chemise, a loose-fitting, unwaisted shape – the exact opposite of his fitted and super-feminine New Look Collection. The chemise dress, *left*, with stand-away neckline and patch pockets, summed up the loose look. BOUCHÉ.

Dior's new coat shape, *above*, followed the lines of his shift dresses. This one in grey wool hung straight at the back but had the look of a two-piece at the front. KLEIN.

Dior's zippy new suit, *right*, full of the vitality of his Autumn Collection. With the chemise, it was an uncanny preview of the youth and freedom of fashion in the approaching Sixties. KLEIN.

Vogue called the dress, *opposite*, 'the most provocative dress of the season'. It was in black *faille* with three roses outlining the dramatically plunging neckline. BOUCHÉ.

Dior's day dresses and coats may have been unfitted, but his evening clothes were voluptuously feminine, with necklines cut lower than ever.

The black silk of the ball dress, *right*, was wrapped around the body to make a daringly low neckline. BOURDIN. Dior's *fichu* collar, *above*, trimmed with a rose, outlined the new neckline of his black taffeta ball dress. BOURDIN.

The chemise for evening – a
shift dress fringed all over
with strands of pearls, *above*. Worn with
large beads and long white gloves. CLARKE.

Making a contrast to Dior's
lush ball dresses in stiff
silks was the elegantly draped chiffon dress,
above, in pale mauve. KLEIN.

Touches of *grand luxe* – a stand
up collar in white mink,
above, matching the white mink pillbox hat.
PRIGENT.

Another Dior chemise dress,
left, looking as young and
free as women felt wearing it. The chignon
hairstyle became very popular. KLEIN.

Vogue chose to feature the white satin ball dress, *left*, 'because it could be one of the prettiest debutante dresses of the season'. The matching coat was in quilted satin with an edge of clipped swansdown. KLEIN.

Vogue celebrated the 10th birthday of the House of Dior with a special portrait of Christian Dior and his favourite mannequin, Renée, *right*. She wore a soft suit in pale green from the *Libre*, or Free, Collection of spring 1957. A spray of Dior's lucky flower was pinned to the lapel. KLEIN.

VOGUE

PARIS
dicte
une
mode
jeune

les
collections
de
printemps
1958

F **600**

NUMÉRO SPÉCIAL · MARS 1958

DIOR
WITHOUT DIOR

The sudden death of Christian Dior was a terrible blow to all at number 30 Avenue Montaigne. They missed him personally: his quiet authority, his gentle manners and his educated view of life. But worse, far worse, was that they were left with an empire and no emperor.

Dior had proved to be much cleverer at business than anyone, including himself, would have guessed. Behind his nice blue eyes there was a clear head for figures of which his father and grandfather, the industrialists, would have been proud. Dior had no romantic delusions about his work. 'The uninitiated imagine a couturier's job to be a mixture of folly, capriciousness, day-dreams, frivolity and money frittered away...' he wrote a couple of years after he opened Christian Dior. 'In reality, behind the perfume, trinkets and model girls, behind all the glamour, there is a serious business in which each metre of chiffon becomes figures, graphs, coefficients, additions, subtractions ... For we are dealers, dealers in ideas, and like any other commercial company we have to sell each season's stock of ideas and balance the books...' (It was this businessman side of Dior that always became so outraged when, despite the strict vetting of audiences, someone would succeed in selling copies of Dior dresses they had not paid for. COPYING IS STEALING said signs in every workroom, and the battle against pirates and plagarists led to a system by which every Dior dress was – and still is – marked with ink that only becomes visible in ultra-violet light.)

Dior's own shrewdness, combined with Boussac's back-up and the skill of Jacques Rouet, the director, had made the House of Dior vastly successful. Early on they decided to capitalize on the fame and glamour of Dior's name, and they became the first couture house to organize licensing agreements by which Dior accessories could be made by other manufactures in other parts of the world. Dior stockings and Dior ties were the first items to be made under license, but by the time Christian Dior died, the list had grown to include gloves, scarves, corsetry, knitwear, lingerie, shoes and costume jewellery.

Dior boutiques selling ranges of ready-to-wear clothes with the Dior label had been opened in Paris, New York, London and Caracas. Christian Dior Furs and Christian Dior Perfumes had both been started in a small way back in 1947, but had grown and grown. (In their first year of production in a tiny factory near Paris, Dior Perfumes had put out 283 bottles of their first fragrance, Miss Dior – by 1971 they were producing 11 million bottles of the various Dior perfumes.)

At the time of Christian Dior's sudden death it was estimated that the annual turnover of the business was some 20 million dollars a year. In the Avenue Montaigne the original three workrooms had multiplied to 28 and there were now departments handling finance, statistics, legal affairs, accounting, licensing arrangements, production and personnel.

Someone had once written, only too accurately: 'A multi-million pound world industry teeters

Y ves Saint Laurent's first Collection
introduced the Trapeze line.
In it he took the loose-fitting look that Dior had started,
to an exaggerated degree. CLARKE.

Yves Saint Laurent surrounded by photographers, *below*. KAMMERMANN-DALMAS. Three examples from Yves Saint Laurent's last Collection, 1960. The puff ball skirt and the snakeskin Rocker's jacket were considered far too young and *avant-garde* for a Paris couturiers Collection. PENN.

like a precariously balanced pyramid, point down, on Dior's head.' Now Dior was dead, and the fashion world and the international Press buzzed with speculation about who would – or could – inherit his crown.

The House of Dior, appalled though they must have been, publicly kept very calm. Soon it was announced that Monsieur Yves Mathieu Saint Laurent, 'who had been part of the team working most closely with Monsieur Dior', would succeed to the empty throne, and that he would be assisted in his formidable task by Madame Raymonde, Madame Marguerite and Madame Bricard – this was the first time their names had been presented to the public.

Like Dior, Yves Saint Laurent came from a family far removed from fashion. His father was a businessman in Oran, Algeria, and young Yves' studies had been directed towards him following in his father's footsteps. But, like the young Dior, he spent every spare moment drawing and designing. At the age of 16 he wrote – out of the blue – to the Director of French *Vogue*, Michel de Brunhoff, asking for advice. De Brunhoff was immensely struck by the talent he could see in the boy's fashion drawings but, though he bought the sketches for *Vogue*, he prudently advised Saint Laurent to complete his *baccalauréat* before coming to Paris and studying fashion design. Saint Laurent duly passed his exams and then came

to Paris where he attended the fashion school run by the Chambre Syndicale de la Couture Parisienne. His first claim to fame came quickly when he won a competition run by the International Wool Secretariat, and soon de Brunhoff, explaining that he had never met anyone more talented than the young Saint Laurent, introduced him to Dior and his future seemed taken care of.

But Saint Laurent was an unknown quantity to the Press and public, and he seemed a curious heir to choose for the prestigious Dior empire: he was only 21 years old, and with his horn-rimmed spectacles and solemn face he looked, as one newspaper put it, 'like a junior bank clerk or a chemist's

assistant'. The journalists did not know how closely Saint Laurent had collaborated with Dior over the past three years, nor that Dior's expressed wish had been to present him to the world as his co-designer.

Yves Saint Laurent had to plunge into his terrifying new job immediately, for the Spring Collection was due to be shown in January, only a couple of months away. It must have been a terrible time for the already nervous young man: his life for the past three years had almost completely revolved around Christian Dior and now his father-figure, his mentor and guide had gone. He had no family in Paris, and although the three mothers, Mesdames Raymonde, Marguerite and Bricard, loved him, the atmosphere at Dior seems to have been oppressive. It was said that Saint Laurent could not even go into a bar by himself without being followed and watched by someone from the house.

However, Saint Laurent pulled through. In January 1958 he showed his first Collection – the Trapeze line. It was a triumph, 'a total, undisputed success,' raptured *Vogue*. The audience applauded almost hysterically, and in an amazing scene, Saint Laurent was called out onto the balcony of the house to wave to the crowd outside, which was chanting his name. Such a thing had never happened, even to Dior . . .

His next Collections, however, were received with less euphoria, and then in July 1960 he showed a daringly *avant-garde* Collection. He shortened skirts to the knee and shaped them like bubbles; waists were dropped to the hips and jackets were cut like motorcyclists' and made in crocodile skin. It was an extraordinarily perceptive Collection to have designed for the dawn of the Sixties, the decade which was to see an explosion of youth, and it had a good deal of influence on the ready-to-wear industry. But it was hardly suitable for the traditional, elegant Dior *clientèle*, who greeted it distinctly coolly.

It was at this point that Yves Saint Laurent was suddenly called up to join the army. Like all Frenchmen, he was eligible for military service, but until now the power of the House of Dior had always managed to have his call-up deferred. Now, it seemed, it could not be put off a moment longer. Perhaps at this stage Saint Laurent's removal from the scene was a blessed relief to the house, who would at least be given a breathing space for a year or so. Life had not been easy at the House of Dior. The stress, as even Dior himself had found, was exhausting: Saint Laurent had lost weight, his hands trembled, and even his most avid supporters (who still thought him brilliant) secretly wondered if he might not be happier designing on his own, away from the pressing obligations of the Dior empire.

It was announced on September 28 that while Saint Laurent was away on military service, the reins would be taken over by Marc Bohan, who had been designing the Christian Dior London Collections for the past two years.

At 34, Marc Bohan was older and more experienced – he had worked for Piguet, Molyneux and Patou – and for a short time had had his own couture house. The Press made much of the fact that he was married with a daughter and would therefore, they reasoned, have a better idea of what women wanted.

But no one could have predicted that Yves Saint Laurent's military service would last less than two months: within a week of joining the army he collapsed with a nervous breakdown and was moved to an army hospital. In November he was discharged from the French army as being medically unfit.

Slowly he began to recuperate. He went to

Marc Bohan at work, *below*. Bohan's tangerine velvet jacket, *opposite*, encrusted with pearls, sequins and costume jewellery with a matching velvet evening skirt. 1961. PENN.

Three examples of the memorable advertisements of Dior products, *right*, drawn by Gruau.

Bohan's young tweed suit, *below*, with a stiff short skirt and matching tweed cap. 1961. PENN.

Diorama
parfum de
Christian Dior

Les
Parfums
Christian D

Miss Dior   Diorama   Diorissimo

Majorca to convalesce and from there, in January of the following year, he told newspaper reporters that he confidently expected to be back at Dior again within a couple of months.

In the meantime, however, Marc Bohan presented his first Collection, which he called the Slim line. It proved to be enormously popular. 'My look was a reaction to what had gone before,' he says. 'I thought women were looking again for a slim, elegant silhouette.' The Slim line was feminine, wearable and most appealing to the Dior *clientèle*, precisely what, in fact, Saint Laurent's last Collection had not been. The decision was made to keep Marc Bohan on permanently and there was now no job for Saint Laurent.

In May that year Saint Laurent sued his former employers for the equivalent of £48,000. Dior defended themselves but were obliged, in the end, to compensate Saint Laurent for the loss of his post. There was much bitterness and many harsh words were spoken, and when Saint Laurent opened his own couture house in January 1962, several of the Dior staff went to join him, including Victoire, the mannequin who had been one of Dior's favourites. Marc Bohan stayed on,

and he has been the designer at Dior now for 22 years, more than twice as long as Christian Dior himself, never failing to produce beautiful, feminine clothes – and, on occasion, influential ones too. Bohan's Collections never ignore the private customers – the 4,000 to 5,000 international women who still buy *haute couture* clothes – and his fans include Sophia Loren, Princess Caroline of Monaco and Bianca Jagger. 'Couture will exist,' he says, 'just so long as the clients do.'

During those 22 years, although Marcel Boussac went bankrupt and died, and the House of Dior changed hands (it is now under the control of the giant textile group Agache Willot, while Christian Dior Perfume is owned by Moët-Henessy), it has never ceased to expand. There are now 38 Dior ready-to-wear boutiques around the world, with a vast list of items sold under the Dior label.

The tight grip that the Paris couture used to have on world fashion has slipped, and ready-to-wear designers have become increasingly important. Ideas still come from Paris, of course, but they also come from America and Britain and Italy and increasingly fashion is springing up from the streets. Packed into the years since Dior died have been a profusion of ideas from varied sources: space-age clothes and mini skirts, trousers and hotpants, the ethnic mixture that was hippy fashion, the universal fad for jeans, the determined ugliness of punk, mini skirts again.

What would Dior himself have thought of it all? Some say that his death was timely and that he would have been lost in the crazy worlds of the Sixties, Seventies and Eighties. 'He would probably have hated what has happened,' says his old friend André Ostier, 'but I can't help thinking that with his flair for fancy dress a part of him would have been greatly amused by the sense of carnival and the feeling of enthusiasm that there is today.' Madame Raymonde declares emphatically: 'If Dior had lived, fashion would not *be* in the state it is in now.'

But let us give the last word to Dior himself. This is what he said in defence of the surrealist fashions of the Thirties, which were about as weird as anything you can see today: 'Fashion is always right – it has a fundamental rightness which those who create it, like those who follow it, often know nothing about.'

INDEX

Bohan's evening dress of ankle-length tiered tulle, *left*, the fitted bodice encrusted with black and gold sequined leaves. 1980. BOMAN.

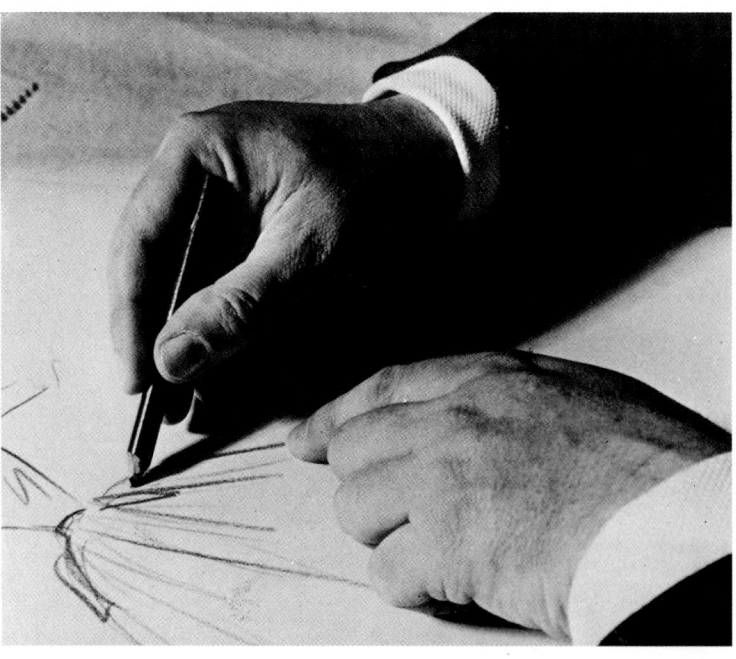